supporting communities affected by violence

supporting communities affected by violence

A Casebook from South Africa

Craig Higson-Smith

Oxfam

facing page: A frightened survivor of communal violence in KwaZulu-Natal, 1994

First published by Oxfam GB in 2002
© Oxfam GB 2002
ISBN 0 85598 477 5

Available from:

Bournemouth English Book Centre, PO Box 1496, Parkstone, Dorset, BH12 3YD, UK
tel: +44 (0)1202 712933; fax: +44 (0)1202 712930; email: oxfam@bebc.co.uk.

In the USA: Stylus Publishing LLC, PO Box 605, Herndon, VA 20172-0605, USA
tel: +1 (0)703 661 1581; fax: +1 (0)703 661 1547; email: styluspub@aol.com

For details of local agents and representatives in other countries, consult our website:
http://www.oxfam.org.uk/publications.html
or contact Oxfam Publishing, 274 Banbury Road, Oxford OX2 7DZ, UK
tel. +44 (0)1865 311 311; fax +44 (0)1865 312 600; email publish@oxfam.org.uk

Published by Oxfam GB, 274 Banbury Road, Oxford OX2 7DZ, UK

Printed by Information Press, Eynsham

Oxfam GB is a registered charity, no. 202 918, and is a member of Oxfam International.

Front cover photograph: Members of the Imbali Peace Committee, KwaZulu-Natal, 1995 (Natal Witness)

Contents

Preface

This book is an account of work in communities devastated by civil violence in KwaZulu-Natal, South Africa. While the stories of these communities have their own particular characteristics and specific concerns, at one level they could easily be the stories of many other communities elsewhere in Africa and the developing world. Whatever the particular political and social dynamics that generate civil conflict, the way in which it changes the lives of individual men, women, and children, breaking up families and destroying community, is universal. For this reason alone, a case study of this kind should be useful. If lessons learned from the KwaZulu-Natal Programme for Survivors of Violence are made available to those working for reconciliation in similar situations in other parts of the world, perhaps communities experiencing civil conflict will receive more effective assistance, more swiftly.

How anything is observed and explained to others depends a great deal upon the person doing the observing. The primary author of this work was one of the founder members of the KwaZulu-Natal Programme for Survivors of Violence (KZN-PSV). He has worked closely with the organisation in various capacities, notably as member and chair of the board of directors, and as executive director for several years. The author's perspective reflects his training as a psychologist with specialist interests in social psychology, community psychology, and the related issues of violence and traumatic stress. Current members and staff of the organisation have contributed substantially to this text, especially Bev Killian, Berenice Meintjes, and Zandile Nhlengetwa. They have each contributed their own areas of experience and expert knowledge. Dr Derek Summerfield made valuable comments on the first draft, as did Suzanne Williams and Nigel Taylor of Oxfam, and Denis Hutchinson. Many other people and organisations have contributed their time, energy, expertise, and resources to the work described in these pages. Oxfam GB has provided financial and technical support, as well as friendship, over many years. This book is the most recent chapter in a long history of collaboration. The debt of KZN-PSV to Oxfam GB, and in particular to Nigel Taylor, the Programme Representative based in Pietermaritzburg, is warmly acknowledged.

While this case study hopes to suggest ways of working in other contexts around the world, there can be no substitute for helpers developing an intimate knowledge of the community in which they are working. Universal prescriptions must be viewed with a sceptical eye. The suffering caused by civil conflict may indeed be universal, but the specific details of history, politics, community relationships, geography, and culture remain crucially important to community work. The need for helpers to develop an intimate understanding of community life is a theme which runs throughout this case study. In the case of the work of the KZN-PSV, an understanding of South Africa's history, and the particular history of the province of KwaZulu-Natal, is necessary before we can begin to understand the history of particular communities, families, and individuals.

One of the features of community intervention is that there is very little in the way of theory and models to guide the community worker. For this reason we tend to borrow ideas from other fields. A good example of this is the understanding of communities as 'ecologies': a central concept of much community work. This concept is borrowed directly from the natural sciences. Of course, human communities have some characteristics in common with natural ecologies, but there are also some important differences. It is dangerous to forget that we borrowed the concept in the first place: we start to mistake the borrowed concept for the actual phenomenon that we seek to understand.

One way of thinking about civil conflict is to consider it as a 'trauma' in the life of a community. Here we are borrowing from the field of psychology. Psychologists define a trauma as a life-threatening event which disrupts the usual flow of life, causing feelings of fear, helplessness, and horror. The outbreak of civil conflict in a community has this much in common with individual trauma. Psychologists argue that traumas can change the fundamental ways in which human beings understand themselves. Any community worker who has worked in situations of civil conflict will observe how the fighting damages the sense of unity and identity of a community. People who once thought of themselves as members of a unified whole are forced to identify with a particular faction within the community, and others who were previously friends quickly become bitter enemies.

If there are these strong similarities between individual trauma and civil conflict, perhaps there are some similarities in the remedies as well. Perhaps as community workers we can borrow some ideas from psychology to advance our own work. Something that is extremely important to most individual trauma survivors is the need to reconstruct and tell their own personal story. As it turns out, communities show the same pressing need to understand in detail what happened in their community, and to have that story known to the world at large. Although this is never easy to achieve, it is fundamental to the rebuilding of communities in civil conflict. South Africa's Truth and Reconciliation Commission is an attempt on a grand scale to explore the country's past, uncover the hidden secrets, and retell the story more truthfully.

There is also a cultural aspect to story-telling. Myths, fables, parables, and other kinds of story are a part of virtually every culture in the world. Although once an integral part of 'Western' teaching and learning, story-telling has sadly fallen into disuse in Europe and North America, and is only recently beginning to regain its rightful place in these cultures. However, this is far less true in the developing world. Many people are very comfortable discussing 'serious' matters through the use of anecdotes and sometimes highly discursive stories. And so, being able to teach and learn through stories may be an appropriate form of intervention for many cultures and may succeed in ways that the more direct and directive 'Western' style of communication may not.

Narratives allow us to understand life more deeply, whether they are ancient myths which contain the heritage of entire nations, personal anecdotes which describe events with special meaning for us, or the histories that explain how we came to be where we are today. These stories play an important role in the lives of us all, and nowhere is this more true than in southern Africa. The universality of story-telling provides a bridge between cultures, a bridge which stands in a place not accessible to either the physical senses or the rational mind alone.

On the surface, this book is the story of a group of people who set about trying to bring hope, healing, and reconciliation to a land at war with itself. It is a story about the people, about the land itself, and about South Africa, a country with a dramatic and continually unfolding tale to tell. And so there are stories within stories, each one serving to bring illumination and deeper understanding to each other. If we are to understand the people of war-ravaged KwaZulu-Natal, we must understand their history and their context. The experiences of people who have survived violence around the world and throughout history tell us how suffering left unacknowledged may be passed on from generation to generation. Examples include families of people who survived the Holocaust or the bombing of cities in the Second World War, and the people of post-apartheid South Africa. South Africa's past is not yet forgotten history: it remains alive in many people's memories. The violence of the past and the present forms layers of experience for many people with whom the KZN-PSV works. One cannot discuss the civil conflict in KwaZulu-Natal without reference to the years of apartheid brutality that preceded it, the years of harsh colonial government before that, and the wars that were fought between Africans, Afrikaners, and British settlers. For this reason, although South Africa's history is well known to many human-rights activists around the world, the early chapters of this case study are dedicated to retelling these stories in brief. Without these bigger stories, the work described in later chapters is without a proper context and loses a great deal of its meaning.

Stories bring people from different backgrounds together, and as such they have served to help the people involved in the work of the KZN-PSV to reach deeper understandings of each other and of their shared world. In a land splintered by a brutal history and on-going civil conflict, learning to understand each other again is a noble aspiration. Furthermore, stories enable us to grapple with our traumatic pasts. Only when we can look back upon the events that haunt us and see them for the history that they are can we begin to speak sincerely of healing. In a world fragmented by violence, the links which stories provide are invaluable. This case study is a story of hardship and struggle, a story of grief and loss, but also a powerful story of love and survival.

The story of South Africa   I

The modern history of South Africa is a story of more or less organised brutality and disastrous social divisions. Of the original inhabitants, the San and the Khoikhoi peoples, few survived the brutality of the early European settlers, who hunted them like animals, or the smallpox which the Dutch, French, and Germans brought with them and to which the native South Africans had no natural resistance. Of those who remained, the vast majority were enslaved by their *boer* (farmer) masters.

The Netherlands, conquered by the French in 1795, ceded the South African Dutch colony to the British empire in order to keep it out of French hands. The first British settlers began to arrive in the Cape within twenty years; eventually slavery was eventually abolished, and English became the only official language of the colony. For these reasons and others, the *boers* became resentful of their British rulers. Several thousand of them trekked north and east into the interior. In so doing, they came into contact with the other peoples who had settled in South Africa and established their own kingdoms. Those who resisted them were defeated. Natal was annexed by the British after a period of bloody conflict with the Zulu people. The British were forced to recognise the independence of both the Transvaal and the Orange Free State. In these independent states, the *boers* began to refer to themselves as the *Afrikaner* nation, and Afrikaans became their official language.

When the gold and diamond reserves of the South African interior were discovered, war broke out between the British and the Afrikaners. By the dawn of the twentieth century, not one of the original African nations retained its independence, and the Afrikaners had surrendered to the British. The Cape, Natal, the Orange Free State, and the Transvaal formed the Union of South Africa, which became a self-governing country within the British empire. This country was founded on a constitution which gave people of European descent (as judged by the colour of their skin) virtually complete and unassailable power.

South Africa's connection with Britain, first as part of the British empire and later as an independent member of the Commonwealth of Nations, continued for the next four decades. However, neither African nor Afrikaans-speaking people were content to be governed for ever by the British. The African National Congress (ANC) had been formed in 1912, with the proclaimed purpose of seeking equality for African people. One year later, Afrikaners established the National Party. They succeeded in having their language officially recognised, which resulted in South Africa having two official languages. Under British rule, the Native Land Act of 1913 began to restrict land ownership by African people, and legislation was passed to create separate services and amenities for black and white people, and to protect the interests of white workers.

The apartheid era

The National Party, with its mostly Afrikaans-speaking support base, came to power in the elections of 1948. Shortly afterwards, the National Party government instituted modern *apartheid* (literally, *apart-ness*), with such notorious legislation as the Prohibition of Mixed Marriages Act and the Group Areas Act, which created separate residential areas for people of differing ethnic backgrounds. 'Homelands' were allocated to particular ethnic groups. The land allocated in this way was for the most part extremely poor agricultural land and far removed from the cities and industrial centres of the country. Many black South Africans were forced to live and work at great distances from their families and were closely regulated while outside their homeland. The indigenous people of South Africa had become aliens on their own land.

With the establishment of the homelands came the most oppressive period of South Africa's history, when homes and communities were destroyed and many people were forcibly moved to other parts of the country. Land and property taken in this way was in most cases sold to white farmers or white-controlled industry. Townships grew up around all commercial and industrial centres, and here black people lived while working in the cities. In addition, hostels were created in many areas and at the mines, where migrant labourers were housed by their employers in extremely poor conditions.

The impact of these forced economic migration patterns on family life is difficult to measure. For generations, South African families have accepted as normal that at least one parent will be away from the family home for extended periods of time. Those women who remained in the rural communities of the homelands were forced to take on the traditional work of men, in addition to their own responsibilities. Many women have supported their families through subsistence farming, in addition to caring for children and aged relatives, while their husbands are away for long periods in the cities. Women who joined the men in seeking work in the urban areas were prevented by law from taking their children with them, and had to leave them behind in the care of siblings or other relations.

Even non-violent political protests were crushed by the government, and the apartheid regime's response to political opposition became more and more brutal. Security forces enjoyed enormous powers, including detention without trial; entry, search, and seizure without warrant; restriction and banning of persons; restriction and banning of organisations, campaigns, gatherings, and publications; the imposition of curfews; and immunity from prosecution. The apartheid regime and its security forces were not afraid to use these far-reaching powers to silence all opposition within the country. As an example of their abuse of power, Coleman (1998) reports that from 1960 onwards 75,000 persons were detained without trial, of whom at least 25 per cent were children and young people, and ten per cent were women. Detention might be in solitary confinement and for virtually indefinite periods, often as long as 32 months. There is clear evidence of torture in detention.

Political repression was not exerted only through the formal mechanisms of legislation and legal security-force actions. With an extensive network of informants and spies, security forces monitored and harassed suspected political activists and their families. There were clear links between homeland police, vigilante groups, hit squads, and the security forces.

Natal Witness

Figure 1 The modern history of South Africa is a story of more or less organised brutality.

Resistance and change

Since the 1960s, the violence implicit in South Africa's social structure has not been limited to a minority group of political activists and the security forces of the apartheid regime. On 21 March 1960, a national demonstration led to the massacre of protesters in the small town of Sharpeville near Johannesburg. Official figures numbered the dead at 69, all killed by members of the South African Police. After almost 50 years of unsuccessful peaceful resistance, the National Executive Committee of the African National Congress sanctioned the use of violence, and *Umkhonto we Sizwe* (literally, *Spear of the Nation*), the armed wing of the ANC, was formed. Nelson Mandela was one of the chief proponents of a move to armed resistance, for reasons described in his autobiography.

> ... I argued that the state had given us no alternative to violence. I said it was wrong and immoral to subject our people to armed attacks by the state without offering them some kind of alternative. I mentioned again that people on their own had taken up arms. Violence would begin whether we initiated it or not. Would it not be better to guide this violence ourselves, according to principles where we saved lives by attacking symbols of oppression, and not people?
>
> (Mandela, 1994: 322)

Sixteen years later, on 16 June 1976, school children in Soweto, a large township in Johannesburg, marched against the use of Afrikaans as a medium of instruction. This march ended (according to official figures) with 128 pupils and residents of Soweto dead.

And yet the facts of these crucially important historical events do not capture the day-to-day life of many people living in South Africa. The following extract is an attempt to describe the everyday life of children in South Africa's townships during this time.

> The world of the township child is extremely violent. It is a world made up of teargas, bullets, whippings, detention, and death on the streets. It is an experience of military operations and night raids, of roadblocks and body searches. It is a world where parents and friends get carried away in the night to be interrogated. It is a world where people simply disappear, where parents are assassinated and homes are bombed. Such is the life of the township child today. (Chikane 1986: 336)

During this time, the struggle against apartheid involved entire communities and was not restricted to a small group of 'politicised' men. When the youth of Soweto marched in 1976, they did so *en masse*, and when the forces of the apartheid regime responded, they did so against the whole community. During this time, with the leadership of the ANC either in exile or in prison, the Women's League of the ANC rose to prominence. Although it was not until very recently that South African women began to organise themselves to challenge gender-related injustices, women's action against the apartheid State has a proud history. With the racial struggle in South Africa reaching its conclusion, the struggle for the emancipation of women is far from over.

During the 1980s, resistance to apartheid continued to grow within South Africa and in many countries around the world. In 1990 the regime realised that change was inevitable, but that its form could still be influenced. The ban on the ANC and many other resistance structures was ended in that year. Within a month Nelson Mandela was released from prison, after almost 26 years, and millions of South Africans dared to dream that real change might eventually become a reality. When change came, it came swiftly. In 1994, all South Africans went to the polls for the first time ever, and the African National Congress swept into power with Nelson Mandela at its head. Since then the country's constitution has been rewritten to protect all its people from unfair discrimination, and the nation is struggling to come to terms with its violent and divided history.

The search for reconciliation

The Truth and Reconciliation Commission (TRC) has spent several years investigating and documenting the seemingly endless lists of brutalities which characterise South Africa's recent history. And yet, in many ways the TRC is a limited medium for reconciliation. Most importantly, it was necessary for the work of the commission to be confined to a very particular period of time in the country's history, namely from 1 March 1960 to 10 May 1994. Events before and after these cut-off dates (which include some important events in the KwaZulu-Natal conflict) fall beyond the brief of the TRC, and as such have received little or no attention. Nevertheless, people everywhere in South Africa are searching for ways to reconcile individuals and groups with each other. South Africa is still beset by many problems, not least of which are the problems of crime and violence. The important difference is that today, *all* South Africans share the right and the responsibility to try to solve those problems.

2 The story of KwaZulu-Natal

KwaZulu-Natal, a sub-tropical land of rolling green hills, lies on the eastern seaboard of South Africa. The province covers only seven per cent of the country's land mass but is home to roughly 21 per cent of the population. With nearly two-thirds of the province's nine million inhabitants living in rural communities, KwaZulu-Natal contains the most densely populated rural areas in South Africa. The large numbers of people living in rural communities, together with a range of other factors, make KwaZulu-Natal in per capita terms one of the poorest provinces in the country. Rural communities in KwaZulu-Natal are characterised by high levels of unemployment (often more than 50 per cent of the working population are unemployed), extreme and widespread poverty, high levels of abuse of alcohol and other substances, and high levels of criminal, sexual, and domestic violence. But the most distinguishing feature of KwaZulu-Natal in recent decades is that it is the province with the greatest incidence of civil and political violence in South Africa. In line with estimates that about 75 per cent of casualties of modern warfare are civilians not directly involved in the combat, much of the violence in this province has taken place at homesteads, in schools, and on the streets.

The rise of the Zulu kingdom

This area was first settled by dark-skinned *nguni* peoples from the north about 2000 years ago. They established various small tribal kingdoms, which shared similar customs and language. For the most part the *nguni* peoples lived in peace and prosperity. Any battles consisted mainly of skirmishes, characterised more by taunts and threats than by extensive killing. In most cases one or other army would be driven off, and the victor would take the others' cattle and capture their women and children. In many cases the victorious tribe would return some of the captured cattle, so that not even enemies would be allowed to die of hunger – in stark contrast to the way in which European settlers who were pushing north and east from the Cape colony were to treat their enemies. Traditional *nguni* culture is highly patriarchal. Even today, families are controlled by the father and his brothers; although there have been female traditional leaders, this is extremely rare.

Figure 2 Map of the Province of KwaZulu-Natal, showing places mentioned in this book.

When the *boers* left the British-governed colony in the Cape of Good Hope, they began to settle in lands which until that time had been entirely under *nguni* control. One of the stronger *nguni* kingdoms was that of the Zulu people. Among the Zulu a powerful military leader arose in response to the growing pressure from the European invaders. This leader was Shaka, who changed the face of society in the region forever and prepared the *nguni* people for war with both the *boers* and the British. He established a standing conscript army and drew the various *nguni* clans into a regulated and peaceful confederacy, strategically strengthened by arranged marriages and alliances.

The relative power of the *boers'* weapons and the extraordinary mettle of the army forged by Shaka are demonstrated in the Zulu nation's most disastrous defeat:

7

The Zulu army, numbering perhaps ten thousand warriors, attacked on the morning of Sunday, December 16, 1838. Wave after wave of them charged the *laager*, to be shot down by the 530 Boer marksmen inside the circled wagons until the adjacent river ran red with their blood. As the plumed warriors began to waver, the Boers moved a wagon aside and a mounted commando rode out to pursue and cut them to pieces. More than three thousand Zulus fell at what became known as the Battle of Blood River. Three Boers were slightly wounded.

(Sparks 1990: 112-13)

The British army followed swiftly on the heels of the *boers* with a new motive: conquest and profit. With the arrival of the British, the pattern of warfare in the region was to change drastically. Sparks (1990: 65) cites the *Grahamstown Journal* of 10 April 1847:

Let war be made against *Kafir* huts and gardens. Let all these be burned down and destroyed. Let there be no ploughing, sowing or reaping. Or, if you cannot conveniently or without bloodshed prevent the cultivation of the ground, take care to destroy the enemy's crops before they are ripe, and shoot all who resist. Shoot their cattle too wherever you see any. Tell them that the time has come for the white man to show his mastery over them.

The Zulu army did not always fare so poorly. At the battle of Isandhlwana in 1878, it destroyed six full regiments of the Second Warwickshire Regiment of the British army; 1800 British soldiers died.

Eventually, however, the Zulu people were unable to withstand the combined ravages of the British army and the *boers*, and in 1879 they were defeated. And yet, by creating the only force in southern Africa to offer any resistance to the British army, Shaka earned the Zulu nation a reputation for aggression and barbarism. This reputation has been adopted as part of Zulu identity and is manipulated for political ends, both by Zulu leaders and by their enemies.

The Inkatha movement

The British named the area Natal and incorporated it into the Union of South Africa. Once the Union had been formed, black people were prohibited from owning property outside the areas designated for them. In the 1960s a 'home-land' called KwaZulu was established for the Zulu people. Chief Gatsha Buthelezi took over its administration, but resisted the apartheid regime's offers of an independence that would have been spurious. At the same time,

Buthelezi began building up the Inkatha movement, which he saw as an 'internal wing' of the banned African National Congress. Inkatha adopted the colours of the ANC flag, used the media to criticise government policies, and called for the unity of black people in South Africa. Buthelezi became a rallying point for the demoralised people, and his popularity soared. As leader of the KwaZulu administration, he was instrumental in the development of the homeland government, including the independent KwaZulu Police force (KP).

However, the mood of the ANC was becoming more militant, and the organisation had committed itself to armed struggle. In contrast, Buthelezi released the following statement to international journalists: 'We cannot afford voluntarily to precipitate a holocaust in this country. We are not afraid to die for our freedom, but we cannot assist the racist regime to make an unarmed people cannon fodder' (interview with *Time Magazine* journalists, cited in Jeffery, 1997: 24). In addition to his rejection of the decision to turn to armed struggle, Buthelezi resisted the ANC's call for international sanctions against South Africa. While this was understandable, given the rural poverty of KwaZulu-Natal, many people felt that he was collaborating with the apartheid regime. The seeds of a most devastating conflict had been sown, and the eventual harvest would be civil war in KwaZulu-Natal. The most comprehensive account of hostilities between supporters of the ANC and the Inkatha Freedom Party (IFP) is provided by Jeffery (1997), from which much of the following account is taken.

IFP vs. ANC

In 1980, four years after the infamous Soweto uprising, students in KwaMashu, north of Durban, staged a protest march. A month later, students in Pietermaritzburg started a school boycott. Buthelezi campaigned actively against these protests, claiming that the students were being manipulated by enemies of Inkatha and the Zulu people. Inkatha supporters and police attacked boycotting schoolchildren in KwaMashu and confiscated 'Free Mandela' posters. This action earned Inkatha supporters the nickname *vigilantes* among the ANC supporters. The student action was not ended, however, and the response from Buthelezi, Inkatha, and the KP was the same. Irregular violent battles continued in the communities around Durban.

ANC members were presented by the propaganda machinery of the apartheid regime as communists bent on the destruction of the civilised, Christian world, and this message was taken up on the ground by Inkatha as well. Communists, known in South Africa as the *Rooi Gevaar* (literally, the Red Danger), were blamed for all the evils of the world, including conflict and poverty in Africa. But while the apartheid regime and Inkatha were portraying the ANC as puppets in a communist strategy to control Africa, the ANC was portraying Inkatha as puppets of the apartheid government. The resulting tensions are illustrated graphically by a young man's memories of his childhood (recorded during an interview with the author).

> ❮ My father used to talk about *inkatha*. He used to call them 'vigilante'. He really hated *inkatha* ... When people from Ethiopia were on TV [during the famine and starvation in that country] ... my mother used to say, 'Just look, if we are also under communists we are also going to be like this'. ❯

The conflicting opinions ascribed to his mother and father describe the political confusion of their generation, neatly summarising the battle-lines of the civil war which would overwhelm this young man's teenage years and result in his taking a life and surviving a bullet wound before his eighteenth birthday.

With the liberation movement irreconcilably divided by these events and ideological differences, the people of KwaZulu-Natal were forced during the early years to choose between the United Democratic Front (which had arisen to continue the work of the banned ANC) and the Inkatha Freedom Party. By aligning themselves explicitly with one or other political movement, people were guaranteed a degree of protection for themselves, their families, and their property. Whole communities were declared 'no-go zones' for opposition groups, and residents in those communities who did not publicly express allegiance to the appropriate movement were driven from their homes by violence and intimidation. In this way the entire province of KwaZulu-Natal was divided into ANC and IFP areas.

The IFP mobilised support on the strength of Zulu nationalism and the dream of a separate Zulu kingdom. The UDF (and thus the ANC) mobilised support on the basis of armed revolution and a unifying democracy. Given these different ideological foundations, it is unsurprising that so many younger people supported the UDF and ANC, while the older generations tended to support the IFP. This created a conflict between generations within all the families and clans of the Zulu people, and did immeasurable damage to the social fabric of the area.

Women in particular were caught on the horns of this ideological choice. Their husbands' authority and position within the community was invested in the traditional culture and structure of Zulu society that was being promoted by the IFP. Their children, who were often better educated and had wider exposure to other systems of government, largely through the media, were often in support of the human rights and democracy promised by the ANC.

As families were torn apart in this way, many women stayed with their husbands and their culture, and their relationships with their children were irreparably damaged.

As the situation worsened, leaders within the ANC and IFP camps established and trained local paramilitary structures. Drawn largely from the ranks of adolescent men in the community, these structures were named Self Defense Units (SDUs) on the side of the ANC, and Self Protection Units (SPUs) on the side of the IFP.

In 1985 violence erupted in Inanda and other communities north of Durban, when Mrs Victoria Mxenge (widow of lawyer Griffiths Mxenge, who was murdered in 1981), a prominent lawyer and leader in the UDF, was shot outside her home. Her killing angered local students, by whom she was greatly respected. They staged demonstrations and school boycotts in protest against the state of emergency. Five thousand people attended Mrs Mxenge's memorial service, held at the Umlazi cinema. Full-scale violence broke out when an *impi* (regiment) of Zulu warriors was transported to Umlazi (an ANC stronghold and 'township' area outside Durban) from Lindelani (an established, peri-urban IFP area) in order to quash the protest action. Civil violence erupted throughout the area, and almost all the shops in Umlazi, KwaMashu, and Inanda were destroyed. The economy of these townships was destroyed within a matter of weeks, and residents were forced to start buying within the city itself, a factor which compounded the poverty of the township communities. (Later, evidence presented to the Truth and Reconciliation Commission revealed the involvement of both Inkatha and State security forces in the Mxenge murders.)

Up to this point, the conflict had been centred around Durban. It was soon to spread to the Pietermaritzburg area. Fighting engulfed the communities here in 1990 and, as the conflict continued, people began to use the word 'war' for the first time.

> Headlines trumpeted the news in huge bold print: 'Natal on the boil'; 'Thousands in *impi* attack'; '"War" in Maritzburg!' ... Among the public at large, and even in the editorial columns of certain newspapers, the prevailing reaction was one of bewilderment. (Kentridge 1990)

Civil war in KwaZulu-Natal

Imbali and Edendale, the largest townships in Pietermaritzburg, had been plunged into civil war, and at last the general public started to recognise the violent conflict between the ANC and the IFP in the province as an important

Natal Witness

Figure 3 Refugees from Sweetwaters find a new 'home': a two-metre-square shack made of wattle and daub. Mr Vusumuzi Khanyile and his family had to flee after a group of Inkatha men attacked their home in 1988.

problem. The conflict continued to spread through the smaller towns and rural communities of the Natal Midlands. Over the next few years, cycles of attack and revenge built up in many areas, and by 1994 there was hardly a community in the province which had not been affected either directly or indirectly by the influx of displaced people searching for safe places to settle. Particularly violent areas included the communities around Pietermaritzburg and Durban, Greytown, Richmond, and Mooi River, as well as the north and south coastal areas.

During this time, at the national level the apartheid regime had begun to negotiate openly with the ANC. That organisation was unbanned, Nelson Mandela was released from prison, and the country headed towards its first democratic elections. But while South Africa was being hailed around the world as a miracle of political transformation, communities all over KwaZulu-Natal were burning.

In the build-up to the 1994 elections, the Inkatha Freedom Party repeatedly changed its decision on whether or not to participate. During this period the violence increased drastically, and at times it was feared that the election

Natal Witness

Figure 4 The township of Slangspruit in the aftermath of civil violence, April 1991

would not go ahead in KwaZulu-Natal because of the continuing conflict in the province, and the very real possibility of a bloodbath on election day. At the last minute the IFP decided to participate in the elections. With the exception of a couple of incidents, polling day passed uneventfully. The results of the election left the ANC in control of the national government and the IFP in control of the KwaZulu-Natal provincial government. The level of violence began to drop immediately.

In the years since then, violence has continued, but at a much reduced level. Despite regular upsurges of conflict in particular communities, continuing dialogue between the two warring groups has led to a gradual reduction in hostilities.

Sadly, in the run-up to the country's second democratic elections in 1999, the emergence of a new political movement called the United Democratic Movement (UDM) contributed once more to outbreaks of violence. The UDM in KwaZulu-Natal consisted largely of disaffected supporters of the ANC. Under a charismatic and controversial leader who had risen to office within the ANC during the years of conflict in the province, the UDM contested the general elections, but it did not receive much support. For much of its life, the UDM has been accused of perpetrating acts of violence. After the assassination of the party's leader in 1998, conflict again erupted around the town of Richmond; but it has since died down again, and with it the future prospects of the UDM.

The legacy of civil war

To date, the conflict in KwaZulu-Natal has claimed as many as 15,000 lives. A further 25,000 people have been seriously injured and disabled. As many as 500,000 people have been displaced from their homes and communities (Jeffery 1997). Although the province is no longer engulfed in civil conflict, the fighting is not over yet. Recent reports of arms-collection points and paramilitary training activities have alerted conflict monitors to the potential for further organised violence in the province (Network of Independent Monitors 2001). The tension appears to be largely due to extreme frustration on the part of traditional leaders (largely IFP supporters) with the government's demarcation of political boundaries immediately before the recent local elections. Many felt this to be a deliberate attempt to dismantle the traditional leadership structure and to deprive these leaders of power and control over their areas.

Aside from these symptoms of organised violence, many reports are received of isolated revenge killings in areas formerly worst affected by the civil war. Most of these attacks are on families perceived to have been involved in the deaths of members of the avenging families during the height of the political violence. This violence also seems to be connected to family feuds extending over several generations. In the more rural areas of the province, much tension is still in evidence along the fault lines of long-running factional feuds, which became politicised during the wider conflict. In one area currently affected by violence, community members describe finding bodies outside their homes each morning. Many of the youth-group members from this area have had to leave the community temporarily, since their newly adopted neutral stance places them at great risk of attack from both sides of the conflict. In a recent group meeting, facilitators enquired about current levels of violence in the area. The members replied, '*This week it is quiet.*' When asked by the facilitator what type of quiet they meant, they replied, '*There are still gun shots every night, but in the morning there are no bodies outside like last week.*' The fact that this violence continues largely unreported is a cause for great concern.

Much of the criminal violence which has been extensively reported in the media seems linked to former political violence. Ex-combatants report their frustration at being trained in paramilitary skills, but having received little formal education. They also describe the disintegration of their families and their sense of alienation from the community following their return from exile and war. Many members of the former nationalist government's security force have now established private security companies, which are alleged to be

Figure 5 Evicted from their home in 1995, Simon and Gertrude Dlamini sit surrounded by their belongings. 'We have nowhere else to go. This has been our home for as long as we can remember,' said Mr Dlamini.

fighting the same war in a different manner. There are recent and increasing reports of security companies actively involved in crime in order to boost their own businesses. Community members complain of biased personnel in the police force, whose members, formerly involved in the political conflict in their areas, now struggle to maintain a neutral stance in responding to crime and violence in their area.

Even without the violence, life is still extremely difficult for the majority of the citizens of the province. The internal structure of many communities was destroyed when people were forced to flee from some areas into others. Nearly an entire generation has missed out on secondary education, the years of adolescence having been spent in fighting. These young people are enormously disadvantaged today in a country with already high unemployment. In KwaZulu-Natal, unemployment figures for young people are the highest in the country, with 45 per cent of African people who are expected to be economically active unable to find work. The local economies that existed before the conflict are having to be rebuilt. In places the infrastructure needed to support the community and the economy has been destroyed. Roads, water, electricity, schools, and clinics have always been in short supply in rural KwaZulu-Natal, but what little infrastructure there was has been destroyed in the conflict. In addition, people have lost an enormous amount of capital wealth, through abandoning family land and through the destruction of homes and other property. Finally, many families are living with the memories of the violent deaths of children and other family members. Some individuals are struggling to cope with the long-term consequences of living under threat and their exposure to acts of extreme violence. These effects include a deep sense of individual and communal helplessness; alcoholism; high levels of aggression, domestic violence, and child abuse; and an increased incidence of emotional problems, including depression and disorders related to traumatic stress, as well as stress-related physical complications. Finally, the rate of HIV infection in the province, substantially greater than in other areas of South Africa, is among the highest in the world. In 1998, 32.5 per cent of women attending ante-natal clinics in the province tested positive for the virus, a figure that has been climbing exponentially since the beginning of the decade. The implications of these figures for the future are daunting.

Initial responses to the conflict in KwaZulu-Natal 3

It commonly happens that societies and governments respond to civil violence too late. The horrifying genocide in Rwanda in 1994 had ended before any kind of effective response was mobilised. Preventing violence should be accepted by community development agencies and governments as the most important intervention required of them. Failure at this level virtually guarantees that marginalised communities will become even poorer and less able to sustain themselves. Whatever lessons we can learn about the prevention of civil violence are therefore of crucial importance.

Since the on-set of civil violence in KwaZulu-Natal, and indeed up to the present day, there has been no effective or organised response from either provincial or national governments. Although it is impossible to be sure that early intervention in the conflict in KwaZulu-Natal would have prevented the escalation into civil war, it is certainly probable. As it turned out, the work of violence prevention, violence monitoring, and peace making at the local level, as well as the work of individual and community healing, was left in large part to non-government organisations. Among these were the existing anti-apartheid groups and human-rights organisations, and church-based and community-based groups. But these organisations too were slow to respond to the imminent civil war. Organised responses began in the late 1980s, by which time the conflict had been brewing for several years, ignored by those not immediately affected. It was not until the escalation in conflict resulted in thousands of ANC and IFP refugees streaming into Pietermaritzburg looking for shelter and safety that any real response was made. It is important to examine honestly the reasons for the delay in response, so that this mistake might be avoided in other places at other times.

The lack of early response

There are four main reasons for the lack of organised response to the early stages of the crisis in KwaZulu-Natal. First, political violence in KwaZulu-Natal disturbed the lives of the poorest, least powerful, and most isolated people, whose concerns are seldom reflected in the media or public debate. On the other hand, it also affected the most politically active, who for reasons of personal safety were prevented from ever speaking about their experiences.

Second, in the 1980s the attention of social activists and progressive health workers and mental-health workers in South Africa was focused on bringing local and international pressure to bear on the apartheid regime. What was happening within and between communities seemed less urgent than the greater struggle. Third, political violence was 'explained away' by some sectors of the media, and by the State propaganda machinery, as 'black-on-black' violence. This violence was portrayed as something inherent to African culture, something which always had (and always would) exist. As such, there was no reason to respond to it.

Finally, the delay can in part be ascribed to simple human optimism and naivety. Although some people understood the deep ideological differences emerging within the province and realised that they could generate dangerous levels of violence, this type of conflict was generally called 'unrest' (as a similar set of problems was called 'The Troubles' in Northern Ireland), and in this way its significance was largely discounted. South Africans did not want to believe that civil war was possible.

Eventually, civil society did respond to the conflict; but, despite high-profile media coverage and on-going public debate and pressure, the government consistently failed to deliver any tangible support to survivors of political violence in the province. The agencies that responded to communities' needs did so with the absolute minimum of resources, mostly generated outside South Africa. Sadly, this situation continues to the present day. Although the Truth and Reconciliation Commission (TRC) did try to achieve a sort of justice, the limited reparations made to victims of violence are a continuance of this sad state of affairs. It should also be noted that the cut-off dates for the TRC (only events between 1 March 1960 and 10 May 1994 were considered) meant that a large part of the conflict in KwaZulu-Natal has never been systematically addressed, and that victims of this violence have very few possibilities for pursuing justice.

It is, however, the purpose of this book to describe some of the efforts that were made to assist communities that survived the civil conflict. Community work in South Africa arises from a long period of social and political activism by courageous people who protested at the brutality meted out by the apartheid regime. In addition, many people involved in mental-health services provided care and support for individuals and families who had experienced detention without trial, solitary confinement, harassment, torture, and other forms of human-rights abuse.

The birth of the KwaZulu-Natal Programme for Survivors of Violence

In 1991, after widespread and escalating civil violence had broken out around Pietermaritzburg, a group of psychologists and social workers turned their attention to what had become the most pressing problem in their region, namely the effects of civil violence. In this way the KwaZulu-Natal Programme for Survivors of Violence (KZN-PSV) was born. These mental-health workers came from a variety of backgrounds but were united in their history of activism against apartheid and their support for human rights. The original group contained about 15 men and women, aged between 20 and 40, some experienced and highly qualified, and others senior students, mostly white people (the ranks of health professionals are still dominated by whites to this day). Most members of the initial group were associated with the universities of either Natal or Durban-Westville.

In the beginning everyone worked on a voluntary basis. Although several of the group were able thereby to further their own studies and qualifications, the central reason for doing the work was that it was the most pressing need expressed by the surrounding communities to which it was possible to respond. When more funds became available, we set about employing full-time community workers, the vast majority of whom were Zulu people from the beneficiary communities.

The decision to turn our attention from anti-apartheid work to an organised attempt to respond to the civil conflict was a difficult one. At that time there were very few indicators that South Africa's political transformation was only a few years away. In 1990 it felt as though the struggle would continue interminably, and that change would not happen within our lifetimes. The fact that the founder members all came from a background of anti-apartheid work was an entirely appropriate and powerful way for the organisation to develop. This is because the history of KZN-PSV exactly mirrors the history of the people whom it aims to assist. Where many of the intended beneficiaries were grappling with the effects of civil violence, against a background of intimidation and violence committed by the State security forces, many of the helpers had themselves been targeted by the security forces and/or had worked with political activists, detainees, people in exile, and their families. This shared history of struggle provided the organisation with its initial contacts, credibility, and trust.

Most importantly, it is necessary to examine the current experiences of the people of KwaZulu-Natal against the background of a long history of poverty, oppression, and State-sponsored violence. The effects of KwaZulu-Natal's history of on-going violence are deep-rooted and cumulative: individuals, families, and communities have been exposed to threats and trauma for generations, with little if any opportunity to recover.

The ideology and philosophy of KZN-PSV therefore have clear historical origins. The organisation is concerned with the psycho-social impact of political violence at all levels of society. The fundamental aim of the programme is to develop appropriate strategies for responding to the needs of communities that have been fragmented by civil violence in KwaZulu-Natal. It is important to note that the aim of the project was never to offer a trauma service to the province. This is the responsibility of the South African government and will depend on its developing a sustainable tax base. An organisation with fewer than 25 staff will never provide a comprehensive service to 8 million people, spread over an area the size of KwaZulu-Natal. The KZN-PSV is a pioneer of innovative intervention strategies and it works to lay the groundwork for more comprehensive State-sponsored services.

Since the emerging problems of civil violence (as opposed to State violence) involved a major reorientation of their work, the founders of the KZN-PSV decided to begin by using intervention strategies and models developed in other parts of the world, particularly elsewhere in Africa and South America. This required a fair amount of reading.

Literature search: learning from others

An extensive literature research revealed very little of direct value. Either nobody was doing any community-level intervention in civil-war situations, or they were doing so but not publishing the results of their work. Later experience has taught us that both suppositions were true. Hardly any genuine community work is done in civil-war situations, and not much of it is documented. All too often, critiques of community work are published which offer very little help to others who need to design effective interventions. This is a big problem for field workers, who are obliged to proceed by trial and error because their peers have not made their own findings and experiences generally available. It is worth noting that this situation has started to change. Today a fairly broad range of work is being reported on, although these reports are mostly descriptive or anecdotal in nature. There is still almost no theoretical guidance for practitioners who are seeking to help to rebuild the social fabric of communities damaged by civil war.

Of course, the literature search was not entirely unproductive. We immediately became aware that there were two broad areas of work which did have relevance to the problems facing communities in KwaZulu-Natal. On the one hand, we explored the literature pertaining to individuals' adaptive and pathological responses to war trauma. On the other, we explored the literature on economic development which dealt with the reconstruction of societies after civil conflict. This literature dealt with the problems of job creation, the rebuilding of vital infrastructure, and so on. A closer look at both these bodies of literature is warranted.

Literature concerning traumatic stress

For many people, the words 'traumatic stress' are equated with post-traumatic stress disorder (PTSD). In fact the literature on traumatic stress is a vast area of work, of which responses to PTSD and other stress-related disorders are only a part. This literature deals with the broad range of human responses to exposure to life-threatening events.

Some Western theorists are very critical of the usefulness of much of the work on individual traumatic stress described in the psychological literature. The work of Derek Summerfield (1996, 1999) is particularly useful in this regard, since it alerts practitioners to the dangers of blindly accepting some of the remedies offered in this literature. Sadly, many African practitioners, desperate for any ideas which might assist in a seemingly hopeless situation, have not been critical enough in this regard. Nevertheless, if this literature is read carefully and applied thoughtfully, it contains valuable insights and information. We would be foolish indeed to discard this work, particularly when there is no ready framework with which to replace it. However, several important concerns should always be borne in mind.

First, theoretical work on traumatic stress is dominated by Western-trained social scientists, working with very specific population groups (college students, veterans of various wars in which the United States of America has been involved, and survivors of the Second World War, notably the Holocaust). Before 1990, virtually no work had been done on the ways in which African people experience, express, and recover from war trauma. This too is beginning to change, as demonstrated by recent congresses of the International Society for Traumatic Stress Studies, which incorporated work from South Africa, Liberia, Rwanda, and Uganda. Furthermore, 1999 saw the first-ever congress of the African Society for Traumatic Stress Studies, which it is hoped will provide added impetus to the work of understanding traumatic stress in Africa. The recent launch of the South African Institute for Traumatic Stress in 2001 is another important step down this road.

A second pervasive assumption in the traumatic-stress literature of 1990 was that traumatic experiences were typically conceptualised as single events occurring within a relatively safe society. Thus it is most often assumed that it is possible to move trauma survivors to a safe place in which they may recover. This is patently untrue for the vast majority of survivors of violence in KwaZulu-Natal and in the rest of the world's civil wars. In these cases, the traumatic event is often only the most recent event in a long history of stress, with all of these events taking place against a background of threat and danger. For this reason, work with victims of motor-vehicle accidents, isolated violent crimes, and natural disasters is severely limited in its application in the civil-war situation. However, reports of work on violent homes and families, gang life in America's inner cities, xenophobia, genocide, and ethnic conflicts are much more informative.

Henderson (1998: 186) describes the experience of civil conflict as 'a complex layering of broken bonds and the accumulation of betrayals of trust'. She explores these ideas further by citing the work of Reynolds (1995), who argues that all families in South Africa 'bear the residues of state policies and actions' and remarks that 'there has been for most South Africans this century no minimal stability for children in families, [or] for families in relation to place ...'. Thus many of the individuals and families who seek out the services of KZN-PSV have survived experiences of family fragmentation and family violence, State violence such as forced removals, detentions, and torture, and most recently civil violence. Furthermore, neither the trauma survivors nor the trauma workers can remove themselves from the dangers of their world for the purposes of healing work. Civil war becomes the context in which healing must take place.

This repeated or continued nature of trauma has in recent years received greater attention. Chikane (1986) introduced the concept of *continuous traumatic stress disorder* (CTSD) as a contrast to the more Western construct of *post-traumatic stress disorder* (PTSD). This concept has been usefully developed by Straker and Moosa (1994). Herman (1992) speaks of *complex traumatic stress disorder*, a term which encapsulates some of the difficult realities of township dwellers in situations of political violence in South Africa, where individuals are exposed to repeated, multiple, and prolonged trauma. Although this work is important in breaking down the assumption that traumatic stress results from a single shocking event in an otherwise safe environment, it does not really begin to grapple with the complexity of the inter-relationships of all these kinds of violence (or threats of violence) occurring simultaneously. The following description of the experiences of one person assisted by the KZN-PSV illustrates this point.

Sibongile (not her real name) was kidnapped from her home with her baby when her community was attacked. During the attack she witnessed the murder of her eldest son. She still does not know where her husband is.

She fears that he too has been killed. She was imprisoned for four months in a metal shack (KwaZulu-Natal regularly experiences temperatures of 40 degrees Celsius in summer) by the paramilitary gang that captured her. She was kept as a sex slave and raped repeatedly by several members of the gang during her imprisonment. Her life and that of her child were constantly threatened. Eventually her captives grew bored with her and released her. Having no means of travelling home, she found her way to a police station in the area. The police were sympathetic to the same political movement that her kidnappers supported, and she was further threatened by officers. Eventually a member of the community put her in touch with KZN-PSV, which happened to be working in that area at the time. KZN-PSV staff were able to return her to her community and help her to obtain the necessary medical care and social support that she and her baby needed.

The stresses involved in witnessing the murders of family members, and having to protect a child while being kept prisoner, raped, and threatened on a daily basis are not captured adequately in the notion of continuous or complex post-traumatic stress disorder. Although not intentional, such labels often imply that the sufferer is unable to cope and is sick; they do not adequately acknowledge the person's resourcefulness in the face of terrible anguish and threat. Where people are returning to the chaotic and frightening world of civil conflict, any intervention that disrupts coping strategies, rather than strengthening them, no matter what they might be, is potentially extremely dangerous. For this reason, some kinds of counselling in this context are hazardous to the client's long-term survival.

It is important to ask whether Western-style psychological theories of traumatic stress have anything at all to offer to agencies working in Africa's civil conflicts. Are there points of contact between the way in which Africans think about war and violence, and the way in which Western psychologists do? Indeed there are several points of congruity, as the following quotations illustrate.

Credo Mutwa is a well-known author and *sangoma* (a Zulu word for a traditional spiritual leader, diviner, and healer) in southern Africa. He explains how African healers understand insanity.

> ... the learning *sangoma* is taught that there are forms of madness which can be cured by certain herbal preparations. There are forms of madness that can also be cured by keeping certain types of metals or substances away from the patients, and there are forms of madness that can be cured simply by changing the patient's lifestyle or by advising the patient to do a certain thing.
> (Mutwa 1996: 23)

In particular, Mutwa identifies stress as a source of many Africans' problems in modern times.

> I was taught, for example, that one of the greatest killers of Africans in modern communities – high blood pressure – is due to the very exacting and high speed lifestyle that our people lead today. If one is an upwardly-mobile black person nowadays, one sooner or later develops high blood pressure, and we are taught that in order to escape this scourge the patient must either change completely or modify his lifestyle. (Mutwa 1996: 24)

Reynolds' interviews with healers in Zimbabwe following the civil war in that country clarify how African healers view the effects of war.

> All *n'anga* I spoke to agreed that the war had disturbed children. They identified three main causes. One was that children witnessed the bloodshed and death. Gushongo said that even if a child only witnessed a killing, the *ngozi* (the unsettled spirit of the one killed) might return to trouble the child, causing him or her to relive the visions, and saying, 'You were there, too.' Evil must be blocked and the cause explained to the parents. Medicine is given to the child to stop him or her reliving the experience. These cases, healers say, are the easiest to treat.
>
> Another cause of distress was from *ngozi* seeking to revenge wrongful deaths. *Ngozi* often attacked children because they were vulnerable and precious family members. In such cases the child is a pawn. His or her well-being depends on the ability of a *n'anga* to reveal the true cause of the child's trouble and on the willingness of the family to tell the truth, pay compensation, or chase the *ngozi* to the killer.
>
> The third cause lay in children's wartime activities. We have seen that as *mujibha* (child wartime messengers who also often served as informers) children held power over others' lives, The world turned upside down: a child could cause an adult's death. After the war children had to live with their consciences. (Reynolds 1994: 64-5)

There are striking parallels between the ways in which Western and African healers conceptualise the effects of war upon people. Are there also similarities in the ways in which these healers respond to people in distress? One of the key components of successful psychological intervention is the therapeutic alliance or rapport that is established between healer and client. Mutwa has this to say about how a traditional healer should behave with a 'patient'.

> A *sangoma*, either during or after initiation, must know how to communicate
> properly with people. He or she must never talk down to people but must talk
> to people at their level. A *sangoma* must never argue with a patient ...
> the *sangoma* must rather keep his or her opinions to herself or himself and
> go along with the patient's beliefs, using them as an effective tool of gaining
> the patient's cooperation during treatment. These and many other important
> rules I was taught as a *sangoma*. (Mutwa 1996: 22)

A key feature of most Western-style treatments for traumatic stress is the
emphasis on retelling the narrative of the traumatic event. This 'ventilating'
process is thought to be fundamental to healing. Similarly, Reynolds describes
the process of the cleansing rituals performed by Zimbabwean healers as
follows:

> ... It is on such recuperative forces that people were able to draw in recovering
> from the wounds of war. The 'legitimate collectivity' must be a knowing
> collectivity. Ritual works by bringing things out into the open and this can
> be a healing process because it is keyed into assumptions about the social,
> moral, and natural orders. 'Exposing to view' cures, but it is not an easy
> spontaneous matter; rather it is a complex process. (Reynolds 1994)

Another important component of psychological responses to traumatic stress
is re-exposure under carefully monitored conditions. Mutwa reports: '... one
discipline ... which is followed by *sangomas* is where a person is exposed
deliberately, under careful observation, to the one thing that he has always
feared in his or her life' (Mutwa 1996: 23).

A further important aspect of Western trauma treatment is working with
the irrational guilt that is experienced by many survivors of violence. Reynolds
records the following work with children in response to their feelings of guilt.

> Immediately after the war Gororo treated many cases of young boys with
> guilty consciences (*zviito zvavakaita*). Each was closely questioned by Gororo's
> spirit. Some were found to have caused people to die but to have had no choice
> given the conditions of war. Yet, some still felt guilty, the spirit revealed.
> The boys were cleansed and given medicine to prevent them from reliving
> their experiences. Gororo warned them that those who lied about their
> experiences during the war would find no relief. (Reynolds 1994: 66)

In fact, there are many striking congruencies between African and Western
work on the effects of war and violence on people and communities. This does

not excuse those Western mental-health professionals who have further victimised communities with their beliefs that all survivors of warfare must be traumatised, incapable of recovery without external assistance – the only effective treatment being particular forms of psychotherapy. Certainly, none of these assumptions is supported by the experience of the KZN-PSV.

The literature of social and economic reconstruction

As the literature on traumatic stress and war trauma raised several important questions for our work, so too did the literature on economic reconstruction following civil conflict, which deals with a range of social problems which are common in Africa. They included widespread poverty, very high rates of unemployment, a breakdown in law and order, and high levels of violent crime. This literature also documents various projects which are extremely impressive in their objectives and their budgets. The scale of this work was not on the level that could be attempted in the early days of the KZN-PSV.

Although economic regeneration was not a reasonable goal for a small group of social scientists on a very limited budget, this literature did provide us with insight into the broader social problems with which we would be forced to contend. It was clear that our work could not focus merely on the internal worlds of trauma survivors, but that we would be obliged to join communities in their frustrating and disheartening struggle with seemingly insurmountable economic and social problems.

Although not sufficient to our purposes either alone or in combination, the published work on individual traumatic stress and economic reconstruction did serve to deepen our insight into the complexity of challenges facing communities who had survived intense civil conflict. Having taken what we could from the available literature, we also realised that we needed a clearer understanding of the position of communities in KwaZulu-Natal. For this we needed to go to the communities of KwaZulu-Natal directly, and learn what we could of the situation on the ground, and possible ways of assisting.

Baseline research programme

In particular we were interested in determining whether civil violence was a priority problem for people in the province. If so, it would be necessary to describe the negative effects of that violence within communities and to pursue ways in which those effects might be prevented and ameliorated. Finally, it was important to know whether the effects of the civil conflict were different from the effects of years of police brutality and oppression under apartheid. With these questions in mind, a range of research projects was undertaken in partnership with the universities of Natal and Durban-Westville. Selected findings from this research programme are presented below.

Getting our priorities right

Our first concern was to find out whether people in KwaZulu-Natal considered the conflict to be a high-priority problem, or whether we as a group of mental health-workers were imposing our own values and concerns. To uncover people's feelings about this question, we carried out a qualitative study in which groups of local people were asked to list and rank what they considered to be the most pressing problems in their communities. The research focused on the concerns of minority groups within the population, since the views of majority groups were expressed clearly through the public discourse. Five focus groups, consisting of elderly people, women, young people, and disabled people, were run in both rural and urban communities in the Natal midlands. Table 1 summarises the results of all the various groups combined.

It is clear from the findings reported in Table 1 that violence is a major concern for the vast majority of people in these communities, ranking only slightly lower than the lack of health facilities and employment opportunities.

Table 1: Minority groups' ranking of problems in their local communities

Rank	Concern	% of groups concerned
1	Lack of health services	100
2	Lack of employment opportunities	90
2	Violence	90
3	Breakdown in education	86
3	Problematic family relations	86
4	Substance abuse	82
5	Shortage of water	69
6	Lack of recreation facilities	59
7	Poor roads and transport facilities	55
8	Problems with pensions and disability grants	52
8	Shortage of housing and land	52
9	Need for electricity	48
10	Teenage pregnancy	38
10	Decline in cultural values	38
11	Problems with sanitation	34
12	AIDS	24
13	Foreigners using scarce resources	10

(Higson-Smith 1995)

This was something of a surprise, since the public discourse at the time was largely concerned with poverty, unemployment, and housing issues. It is only recently that violence has become a central element of public debate in South Africa. Interestingly, family violence was coded under 'problematic family relations', which was also a high priority. Thus problems relating to violence are accorded a high priority among people in communities of KwaZulu-Natal; when an appropriate channel is provided, this need is clearly expressed.

As expected, women and men accorded very different priorities to certain issues. Since it is commonly men who control public debate and policy on community-related issues, the researchers were very interested to see the different concerns of less powerful groups, particularly women, who comprised the numerical majority of these communities. The women's groups tended to focus on the lack of facilities (particularly health care and clean water), violence in the community, and problematic family relationships. The question of employment opportunities followed these three.

Descriptive studies of communities in civil conflict: Richmond and Imbali

'Violence' was too broad a category to help us to understand exactly what problems were of concern to people, and how common these problems were. To learn more about this, the KZN-PSV conducted a needs-assessment exercise, focused particularly on problems relating to violence in the Richmond area. While it is true that Richmond is one of the communities that has suffered most in the civil conflict, there are at least ten other large communities whose violent history is comparable, if less sensational.

Richmond is a small community roughly 80km south-west of Pieter-maritzburg. It is situated in beautifully green hill country and survives largely on the strength of agriculture and timber. The surrounding countryside is covered with farmland and plantations. The smaller town centre (populated largely by white South Africans) is surrounded by township and rural communities, whose inhabitants are employed within the town and on the farms and plantations.

The townships consist of tightly packed homes, and in some areas shacks, and are very densely populated. The dirt roads are frequently muddy and usually crowded with young children playing and teenagers whiling away afternoons after school. At night the communities are poorly lit and potentially dangerous. The townships around Richmond are closely controlled by the political parties in the area, notably the ANC and UDM. The police based in the town have limited power in the township and have often been accused of collaborating with one or other political party in the area.

The rural communities around Richmond consist of clusters of between ten and twenty traditional Zulu huts, dotted around on the hillsides. Typically a single dirt road, often in poor condition, leads to the village, where visitors are met by a group of young children and a couple of dogs. Each village is controlled by an *induna* (a traditional leader), who is accountable to the *nkosi* (chief of the area). Several extended families typically make up a small village, and it is common for most of the men to be away from home for long periods of time. These men find work in the larger cities of KwaZulu-Natal and South Africa, returning only for short visits on public holidays and when they have leave from work.

These rural and peri-urban communities have been the sites of on-going violence between the IFP and the ANC (and more recently between the ANC and the UDM) since the late 1980s. On repeated occasions, streams of displaced people have flowed into the Richmond town centre, to camp on sports fields and open ground and watch helplessly as smoke rises from their burning homes on the surrounding hillsides.

The aim of this study was to determine the extent of the need in the Richmond area, so that an appropriate intervention could be planned. Through the local office of one of the political parties, families in the communities were invited to meet with staff of KZN-PSV to discuss their experience of violent incidents. A total of 218 heads of household came to the meeting and waited patiently while we tried to interview each one. In many cases, these heads of household were women whose husbands had been killed, or were away in Pietermaritzburg, Durban, and Johannesburg. Each of the people to whom we spoke was representing (on average) three children and two other adults. Tables 2 and 3 summarise some of the types of violent event which these families had endured, and the mental-health problems which the individuals reported as results of those experiences. With these levels of exposure to traumatic events, the available psychological literature predicts high levels of trauma-related distress. As Table 3 demonstrates, these predictions were accurate. However, we should not make the mistake of assuming that this suggests that the *meaning* of the traumatic events or the resultant physical and emotional changes is the same as for other populations.

Table 2: Proportions of families experiencing violent incidents

Stressful life event	% experienced
Home burned down	81
Lost all property	79
Shot at or attacked	57
Wounded	19
Witnessed killing of family member	11

Table 3: Reports of trauma-related distress

Stress-related symptom	% experienced
Cry very often	49
Nightmares	38
Difficulty falling asleep	34
Unable to concentrate	19
Feel sad all the time	15
Problems with memory	13
Feel angry all the time	11

These figures reflected the histories and current mental health of about 1300 people (218 heads of household x 6 individuals per household). It is worth noting that, since the study was conducted through a particular political party office, only about half of the total community of survivors of violence would have participated. The findings clearly demonstrated the need for immediate intervention in this community, as well as other communities which have experienced similar amounts of violence.

These findings were confirmed by another research project conducted by members of the KZN-PSV management committee. These researchers investigated the experiences of junior-school children in Imbali, an urban community close to Pietermaritzburg. Imbali is a large, well-developed township with many tarred roads, a nearby hospital, several schools of all levels, and even a teacher-training college. It was one of the communities around Pietermaritzburg which experienced the brunt of the political conflict in the early 1990s.

The sample for this study consisted of 300 children in Standards 2 and 3 from five schools. The majority of subjects were between nine and twelve years of age. The children were assessed by means of a Life Events Scale, a Symptom Checklist, a Demographic Questionnaire, a Human Figure Drawing, and a Projective 'Life Events' Drawing.

In terms of exposure to violence, it is clear that in the Imbali community many children have been exposed to many potentially traumatic events. Three-quarters reported direct exposure to violence, and virtually all of them reported indirect exposure. Tables 4 and 5 contain a selection of the results.

Table 4: Imbali children's direct exposure to violence (%)

Witnessed a person being assaulted	46
Own house raided by security forces	32
Witnessed someone being killed	27
Own house attacked or burned	15

Note the different types of violence witnessed in the township environment, compared with the more rural environment of Richmond. Close to the cities, and especially in areas in which students were actively protesting against the apartheid government, police and security-force action was common and violent.

Table 5: Imbali children's indirect exposure to violence (%)

Prevented from attending school due to violence	68
Houses in the area attacked or burned	64
Family member arrested	39
Had to move house in order to be safe	26

As would be expected, given the high incidence of traumatic events, high levels of emotional distress were also observed. The data from the symptom checklists are supported by the data from the projective drawings. More specific data are reported in Table 6.

Table 6: Symptoms of distress among Imbali children (%)

Wake up at night and can't go back to sleep	66
Often feel sick and have pains in the body	55
Don't fall asleep easily at night	54
Feel tired a lot of the time	46
Places avoided due to association	41
Difficulty remembering things	33
Feel frightened a lot of the time	23

In all our work so far, we had clearly demonstrated the urgent and widespread need for social services. However, we had failed to show that communities that had experienced civil violence were in worse shape than the rest of South Africa's communities which had suffered under colonial rule and apartheid for generations.

Comparative study designed to isolate effects of civil conflict

For this reason a study comparing two communities, only one of which had been directly affected by the more recent political conflict, was undertaken – although it was difficult to identify a community untouched by the civil violence, since even those in which no fighting had taken place had absorbed people fleeing from more violent places. Finally a rural community which had established itself around a mission station in the Midlands was chosen as a community virtually untouched by the conflict between ANC and IFP supporters. A comparison between this community and a community that had experienced a great deal of civil conflict was carried out. In this case, people in both communities revealed a high incidence of emotional distress, but in the community which had been directly affected by political violence the incidence was significantly greater. Abuse at the hands of the apartheid government and involvement in resistance to apartheid did not break up families and communities in the same way that the ensuing civil conflict did. Although fear and violence were part of both communities' daily existence, the social fabric in the community exposed to internal conflict had been damaged far more. This research is important, in that it clearly identifies the communities of KwaZulu-Natal and others where there has been civil violence as being in *special* need of services for survivors of violence.

Putting the research to use

One of the criticisms often levelled against social researchers is that their findings seldom find their way into practical work with people in need. The research conducted in the early days of the KZN-PSV was put into use in multiple ways.

- First, the research demonstrated that there was an expressed need on the part of rural and urban communities for positive responses to civil violence. This was not an agenda imposed by middle-class, white psychologists and social workers. It was the starting point for all the work that took place over the next decade and continues today.

- Second, despite arguments that community resources would be sufficient to cope with the challenges of internal conflict, this was clearly not the case. Many months after particular incidents, local economies were not reviving, displaced people were not returning to their homes, families had become divided, and adults and children were still experiencing marked emotional distress.

- Third, the baseline research enabled the members of the KZN-PSV to form some idea of the size of the problem, and to identify particular social groups and geographical communities at risk. Although initial concern centred on children and adolescents, it soon became clear that young people in schools were relatively protected, whereas youths who had left school to participate in the fighting were most at risk. Women working in local communities were identified as an important resource for building peace and development projects. At the time, danger areas were the communities around Pietermaritzburg and Durban, as well as Richmond and Greytown in the Midlands. As the years passed and the fighting moved around, greater attention needed to be given to the areas of the North and South Coast regions.

- Finally, the research, with its attention to facts, figures, symptoms, and numbers of people in distress, convinced international donors that this small group of mental-health workers had the capacity to manage a decent-sized project and were committed to doing the work carefully and thoughtfully. In this way the research paved the way for the organisation's first funding contract, made with the Royal Danish Embassy. This initial grant paid for the first two full-time employees and the establishment of offices in Durban and Pietermaritzburg for two years. During this time the KZN-PSV was able to demonstrate its capacity further and attract donations from other human-rights and health organisations, mostly in Europe. It was after these first couple of years that the organisation began to work with Oxfam GB. Increased interest in the organisation's work gradually enabled the KZN-PSV to extend its complement of full-time staff to more than 20 people. In addition, a number of students work with the employed staff as volunteers and under intern-training and practical work-experience arrangements. This increased capacity has enabled the organisation to provide more comprehensive services in a greater number of target communities.

Designing strategies for intervention

What the research did not explore was how best to proceed with intervention. In the beginning the organisation's staff and volunteers tried whatever seemed likely to work, in order to help the people of KwaZulu-Natal. We entered into an on-going process of negotiation and consultation with communities. This took the form of formal meetings with community leadership (including political leaders, local government councils, development committee, traditional leaders, and other internal community structures). In order to deepen the level of consultation, presentations and discussion regularly took place at public meetings in an attempt to find out what the people in the community were most concerned about, and how they thought the organisation might best be able to assist them. Slowly partnerships between the leadership and people of the beneficiary communities and the organisation were established.

Out of these meetings developed the organisation's early projects. This work was designed to help teachers to identify and assist children in their classes in need of special assistance; also it aimed to work with militarised youths, to start peace talks at the local level and develop income-generating and work-skills training to integrate them back into their communities. Negotiation and peace work with local leadership was attempted, as were camps for youth leaders, youth groups, women's groups, peer-counselling programmes and the like. Some of these projects were extremely successful, and others less so. These and other activities are described in more detail in later chapters. In each case the work was based on established principles of community work.

This early period was frustrating, with projects taking a long time to become established, and making only moderate impact upon the community. The reasons for this are multiple and complex; they relate to the particular social climate of KwaZulu-Natal at the time. Two important factors deserve mention. Firstly, the conflict between the ANC and IFP had not reached a point where useful and sustainable community-development work was possible. On more than one occasion, the results of months of community-building work were destroyed by a single attack on that community. Once again people would flee, homes would be destroyed, businesses would close, and the feelings of helplessness and desperation would return. However, the relationships that the people of KZN-PSV were developing in those years would be the foundations upon which later success would be built, even if they did not produce concrete results in the short term. In 1998, when the author left the KZN-PSV, a community representative made a speech at a farewell function. She ended by saying, '*What made the difference is that the people from Survivors of Violence kept coming back, even when things were really bad for us.*'

Secondly, the organisation lacked a unifying model which would help us to understand how community dynamics change in situations of civil conflict, and how these altered dynamics must determine the most effective strategies for intervention. The staff and volunteers needed a plan to direct their actions in a co-ordinated and effective way. Some framework for understanding community dynamics in civil conflict is required to guide intervention. While there are many ways of conceptualising civil violence, the model developed and used by the KZN-PSV has proved very useful. It is presented in the next chapter.

4 Understanding civil violence

The need for a framework of intervention

Good intentions cannot sustain effective intervention. Without a framework to assist community workers' understanding of the situation in which they are working, and a clear intervention strategy to guide them, helpers rapidly become burned out, disillusioned, and even traumatised. There are many reasons for this, but chief among them is the need to make important and difficult choices.

Imagine a situation in which a pair of skilled community workers drive out to a particular place for a meeting with local leaders to discuss the possibility of running a project in that community. Upon arrival, they notice a little girl of about 10 years old, playing alone in a ditch containing filthy water. She is clearly malnourished and has several open sores on her legs and arms. In addition she is playing near the main road, where she is at risk from passing traffic, as well as adults who might wish to hurt her. If the community workers stop the car and talk to her, she will take them to her home. It is not unlikely that they will discover that she has never known her father, and that her mother works in Durban during the week. She lives with her aunt – who, the community workers quickly learn, is depressed and alcoholic and cannot care for herself, much less the child. The child should be at school, so perhaps teachers can help. The community workers are pleased to see that the school is actually open, but not surprised to find that the child has not been attending. Upon talking to the teachers, they discover that they are deeply demoralised: they have been sent from another community, and local parents refuse to discuss their children's needs with them. The community workers arrange for the child to be placed in one of the classes. Whether she will attend is uncertain. The child's sores need to be attended to urgently, but the mobile clinic is not due to arrive for another two days. The community workers search for someone in the community to promise to take the child to the clinic when it arrives. Finally, perhaps it would be possible to get a welfare grant to assist the aunt in feeding the child. The application process is long and complex, requiring the involvement of the biological parent. The community workers set about trying to find the child's mother … and so it goes on.

The first difficult choice was whether to stop and help the child or to drive past. Had the community workers realised that there were probably several hundred children in similar circumstances in the community and had they decided instead to intervene in a different way, they would have had to accept that that particular child's circumstances were unlikely to change in the short term. Next they would have to decide whether to start a support group to assist depressed and alcoholic women, or an income-generating project for women, to enable mothers to earn income within the community, or a programme to encourage parents' interest in the school, or a campaign to open a full-time clinic in the community ... and so on.

For each person in the community, there is a whole new set of problems and possibilities. Workers from the factory which closed down when the fighting started have skills but no jobs, and they would like to start their own local business. They need a start-up loan and skills training in small-business management. Local leaders are not managing to contain small outbreaks of fighting within the community and would like to learn how to handle conflict more effectively. The young men who are doing the fighting have missed out on five years of education and would like to develop their literacy and language skills, to have a better chance of getting places on carpentry and building courses.

The two community workers are presented with an overwhelming catalogue of problems and possibilities for intervention. They are forced to make difficult choices. For every problem that they choose to focus on, several others must be ignored. In this situation it is easy to become paralysed and end up doing nothing helpful at all, or to make frantic efforts to manage each problem as it emerges. But this is impossible, and once again the community workers' efforts are ineffective. Some overarching plan is necessary to guide the work in a particular community.

Four questions that a guiding framework must address

The following are four crucial questions which are virtually impossible to answer without some kind of guiding framework.

In which communities should attention and resources be focused?

Every year decision makers in the KZN-PSV are confronted with requests from community leaders and representative structures throughout the province for particular kinds of work in their area. It was not always like this. Descriptions of the organisation's work passed by word of mouth among areas, and today KZN-PSV is in demand to run projects in various communities. For a non-government organisation of extremely limited means (relative to the need), very difficult choices must constantly be made. To what extent should the resources be allocated to the most violent communities, where the needs are greatest, but the cost of meeting them very large, and the risk of failure greater because of the instability of the area? To what extent should resources be concentrated in particular communities? We know that if we spread resources further, we can offer our services to a larger number of people. We also know that when multiple projects are run simultaneously within particular communities, they support each other, and change becomes sustainable.

At the same time, decision makers must be transparent in their deliberations and serve all parties in the conflict equally. These decisions, with their far-reaching implications, become impossible, and in the end arbitrary, unless there is some kind of framework to guide intervention.

What intervention strategy is best suited to a particular community?

Assuming that a particular community has been selected for work with the KZNP-PSV, what is the best way to proceed there? We are acutely aware that every community has its own 'personality', comprising a particular history, local dynamics, the available resources, and the most pressing challenges. To expect to find a single 'one-size-fits-all' intervention is unrealistic and inappropriate. Nevertheless, concrete and challenging choices must again be made. Resources allocated to reintegrate para-military forces in the community cannot simultaneously be used to train lay counsellors.

Some clear framework for understanding communities recovering from civil violence is needed in order to set the goals for appropriate intervention, and to guide the search for effective and efficient strategies.

How to prevent burn-out and secondary traumatic stress among field staff?

Work in conflict situations has a notoriously high burn-out rate. The costs to the individual and the organisation are great and, as far as possible, must be minimised. Community workers in the situation described at the start of this chapter are subjected to almost unbearable risks to their own personal safety, and it is not surprising that many people cannot endure the work for very long.

One of the most important reasons why community workers leave the sector is that they feel overwhelmed by the needs of community members, and are unsure whether what they are doing is making any difference to people's lives at all. How can the work be designed in such a way that the benefits start to become obvious?

Another source of stress is having to make difficult choices. This is inevitable, but where the community worker is guided by a good model of intervention which clearly outlines his or her role and responsibilities within a particular community, some of these feelings of being overwhelmed or ineffectual can be dealt with. A clear set of objectives which make sense to the community workers and provide a sensible strategy for bringing about lasting change enable them to engage effectively with problems facing the local population.

Finally, the organisation has a responsibility to protect the physical and emotional well-being of the workers. How can this best be achieved? How do those responsible for the organisation know when they are doing enough to protect their staff and volunteers?

What limits should be set on involvement with a particular community?

Once work has started in a particular community, more and more opportunities for intervention open up. The temptation is to keep on allocating ever more resources to that community, because the work is progressing well, trust has been established, and ready-made opportunities for change can be maximised. However, the danger lies in neglecting other potentially more needy communities because it is easier and more rewarding to work in contexts where the organisation already has an established presence. At some point it is necessary to end projects and to move on to work in other areas. How are community workers and decision makers to decide when the level of resources allocated to work in a particular area is sufficient, and to judge that additional resources would be better spent elsewhere? What are the markers to indicate that the intervention has grown to a size at which real change is forthcoming?

This decision requires the work to be constantly evaluated. The problem of evaluating interventions is crucial. Community work costs a great deal of money. The work of the KZN-PSV, with its long-term commitment of staff time to communities, is no exception. These resources might have been spent in many different ways. It is necessary to demonstrate effective utilisation of funds and, where the intervention has no lasting effect, to change the intervention strategy. But how are we to measure the effect of an intervention?

Civil violence affects people and communities in multiple, inter-connected ways. Similarly, any intervention within a community had many differing impacts, some directly observable and some more subtle. Naive attempts at evaluation tend to measure factors like the number of violent incidents per month, or the number of deaths per month, or the prevalence of trauma-related symptoms in a random sample, and so forth. In a complex and unstable community, each of these indicators is likely to be influenced by a range of factors, the least of which might be the actual intervention. Does this mean that the intervention is having no effect at all? Not necessarily. What it means is that we have not found appropriate ways of measuring the effects of the intervention. Thus, a guiding framework must tell us how to measure the impact of our work as well.

Finally, we need to know what signals the successful completion of the work in a particular community. Most of the communities with which the KZN-PSV is involved are extremely poor and have been so since the times before the civil conflict in KwaZulu-Natal began. The aim of the project is not community economic development. However, the challenges presented by civil conflict are often difficult to distinguish from the challenges created by years of living under apartheid, and before that under colonial rule. A guiding framework must help the community worker to distinguish between the results of chronic poverty and the results of civil violence. In this way, when a community has developed the capacity to thrive again following civil violence, a decision to stop working within a particular community can be made.

Clearly a model which answers all of these questions would be a powerful tool for the KZN-PSV, but only if it emerged from within the organisation and its on-going work in communities in which the civil violence had taken place. Thus, the way in which the entire organisation works must be geared towards thinking and reflecting, and not only towards action and community work. How this was achieved is the subject of the next section.

Establishing an organisational climate conducive to the development of a model

The business of model building can be bewildering and daunting, and is not easily achieved when personnel are feeling stretched to the limits of their tolerance by the conflicting demands of their target communities and their employer. On the one hand, field personnel are determined to assist the communities in which they are working, and they rely on the technical and emotional support of the organisation to do this. On the other hand, their work must be constantly assessed, and methods of intervention changed, if progress in model building is to be achieved. Without an appropriate organisational climate, this tension becomes extremely difficult to manage. The KZN-PSV recognised the need for the following steps in order to create a suitable climate for thinking critically about civil violence and community-intervention strategies.

- Firstly, the intended beneficiaries of the work must be encouraged to reflect critically on the aims, strategies, and outcomes of specific projects and the organisation as a whole. If the beneficiary community is well represented in the management of the service, a strong critical voice can emerge within the organisation. Of course, this is not without its difficulties. The KZN-PSV operates with an executive committee, consisting of experienced, professional service providers and representatives of the beneficiary communities in roughly equal measures. These two groups have entirely different histories, social and economic backgrounds, and understandings of communities in crisis and the work of the organisation. Dialogue between these groups is, therefore, extremely difficult to facilitate. However, some of the most constructive criticism of the organisation's work has come from this source.

- A second important strategy to enhance the model-building function of an organisation is to encourage field and office personnel to reflect critically on all aspects of the organisation's functioning. This is greatly facilitated by a management style which allows all members of the organisation to express their views critically. Positive reinforcement to complement critical comment is important, particularly in environments where workers have a strong emotional attachment to their work and the people with whom they are working, and may thus find it difficult to accept constructive criticism. Personnel should also be encouraged to contribute to debate about the way in which the organisation itself is run. How people are managed directly affects the way they work in the field.

- Furthermore, by providing an example of sustainable and self-critical organisational process, the development agency can help community-based structures and projects to achieve their objectives more effectively. In the same way that the staff and board of the KZN-PSV are finding their way without benefit of a 'road-map', many community structures are trying to solve new problems without the technical expertise or experience for the task. Community projects also need to be constantly and constructively assessed in order to maximise their effectiveness and efficiency. Through all their work, the staff of the KZN-PSV remain aware that the way in which they interact with each other and run their organisation serves as a model for many others who are struggling with similar issues within local community structures.

- Finally, it is important that an on-going cycle of critical evaluation and development of intervention strategies is developed. In the KZN-PSV this is understood as an action-research cycle. Thus all staff understand that on a quarterly basis they are expected to produce progress reports, and that on a six-monthly basis the organisation will assess the effectiveness of current strategies and, where necessary, will change strategies. This way, instead of staff feeling that their supervisors are always 'shifting the goalposts', staff feel that they and their supervisors are constantly grappling with the difficult and changing challenges that confront the beneficiary communities.

Since its beginnings, the people involved with KZN-PSV have struggled with the question of how best to assist communities of KwaZulu-Natal, given the very few resources available. The cycle of assessing work, identifying problems, formulating and testing solutions, and further assessment continues. However, as the team's understanding and intervention strategies have improved, the degree of change required in each cycle has become less. This is an indication of real progress.

Some of the answers that KZN-PSV has found are presented below, not because we believe they are necessarily applicable to all communities that have survived civil conflict, but because they are the product of a valuable process which we recommend other practitioners to employ, and because this model may assist other practitioners in their struggle to help other communities to find solutions to similar problems.

A model for understanding the effects of civil violence

When a field worker sits down with people from a community that has survived civil conflict to discuss how the violence has changed things in the community, he or she is typically bombarded with an overwhelming range of problems and concerns, some of which were described at the beginning of this chapter. This all becomes easier to cope with if community life is described in terms of ecological systems, an approach first used by Bronfenbrenner (1979) in developmental psychology to describe the different worlds of children, but since used in a wide range of other social arenas.

Depicting the world as comprising four distinct levels of functioning helped the staff and volunteers of the KZN-PSV to grapple usefully with otherwise overwhelming and confusing social problems. The four levels are those of *individual functioning; small-group functioning* (including families, classrooms, paramilitary units such as self-defence and self-protection units in South Africa, gangs, and prayer groups); *community functioning* (with communities being defined geographically); and the functioning of our *society in general*. This is represented diagrammatically in Figure 6.

Figure 6: A systemic model of civil violence

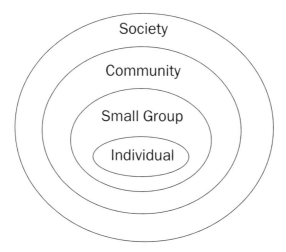

Now instead of asking one broad question, community workers have four more focused questions to ask members of the community in which they are working. The first one would be, '*How has violence changed the lives of individual people?*'. This is immediately a more manageable question, and the answers are not as impossibly overwhelming. The next question would be, '*How has violence changed the way small groups in the community function?*', and so forth.

Of course, in order to develop a full picture of the effects of civil violence, both the community workers and the local people must come to realise how the effects at one level affect all the other levels of the community as well. As the picture develops, a structured understanding of the complex effects of civil violence emerges. The following accounts of actual events illustrate this point.

When the home of a minister of religion is destroyed and he and his family are forced to relocate, the effects are multiple and inter-related. Firstly, there are the effects upon the minister (individual) and his family (small group). Secondly, there are the effects upon the prayer groups that operate from the church (small group), which cannot continue to operate. Thirdly, the community loses the important resource of a spiritual leader and healer within the community (community-level effect). In turn, the individuals who would have attended church and received emotional and spiritual support are left to fend for themselves (more individual and family-level effects), and there is

43

nobody to conduct funerals and other ceremonies within the community. Finally, events affect other systems as well. The minister and his family may become added burdens on the resources of whichever community they move to (a couple of extra places in the school, more competition for jobs, etc.).

Similarly, it sometimes happens that a young person who has been involved in a paramilitary group is accused by its members of 'selling-out' to the enemy. This is a particular danger when starting peace-making projects which involve meetings between warring combatants. Since many youths have been murdered for this 'crime', such accusations are extremely frightening and traumatic (individual effects). However, such victimisation is seldom restricted to the individual, and very often family and friends are similarly threatened. In some cases, families are forced to protect themselves by turning against the individual or fleeing from the community (small-group effects). Such suspicion and threat within communities makes individuals very reluctant to be seen with people and agencies from beyond the community. This isolates the community from important developmental opportunities (community effects). Where this situation exists in numerous communities, social services, including health, welfare, education, and security, become compromised (societal effects).

Going further in the analysis of the effects of civil violence on communities, we focus on each level in turn. If one lists all the various effects of civil violence at a particular level, one finds that it is possible to classify them all into two inter-related categories. The effects of violence at all levels are all associated with either *disempowerment* or *fragmentation*. These two words are central to the way in which the staff of the KZN-PSV understand the effects of civil violence, and so they demand more careful discussion.

Disempowerment

The word 'disempowerment' has acquired many different meanings in different contexts and has therefore lost some of its usefulness. In our case, it refers to the way in which civil violence prevents individuals, families, and other small groups, as well as community structures, from fulfilling their function or original purpose. For example, not having a safe place to play is disempowering for children whose function is (in part) to play freely and develop their full intellectual, physical, and emotional capacities. This is an effect at the individual level. When parents have to devote their energies to basic survival strategies, they are disempowered in fulfilling their role as parents and guardians of the family. This is a small-group effect. Similarly when local political parties take over the role of ensuring the safety of the community (through para-military forces, for example, or 'kangaroo courts'), the local police are unable to carry

Figure 7: Consequences of civil violence, and aims of intervention

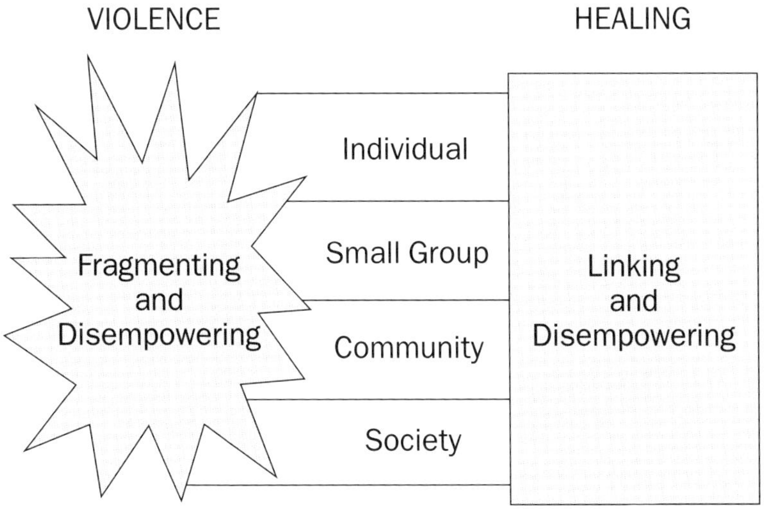

VIOLENCE   HEALING

Fragmenting
and
Disempowering

Individual

Small Group

Community

Society

Linking
and
Disempowering

out their intended function. This is a community-level effect. When seen in this light, a wide range of the stated effects of violence can be understood as disempowering in one sense or another.

Fragmentation

'Fragmentation' refers to the breakdown in communication which happens between individuals, within small groups, and within and between community structures, as a result of violence. The Zulu people have an important saying: *umuntu umuntu ngabantu*, literally translated as *a person is only a person with other people*. In other words, it is only within a community that a person can be a real person, through contributing to the greater good, and it is the community which in turn adds human qualities to a person. To express it another way, society is not merely the sum of individual lives: it is much more than that, and unless this is constantly borne in mind, services are unlikely ever to address the effects of violence upon human relationships and organisations.

When children are sent away from their homes to stay with relatives in safer communities, the family is fragmented (small-group level). When community structures become so distrustful of external service agencies that those agencies are prevented from working in the area, the entire community is fragmented (community level). Those effects of violence which are not disempowering are fragmenting.

Linking and empowerment

Conceptualising violence in terms of disempowerment and fragmentation provides us with a framework to understand these complex social dynamics. Similarly, by planning our interventions around the contrasting concepts of *empowerment* and *linking*, we can ensure that we consistently work in a therapeutic and developmental way. In other words, healing is understood to be achieved when individuals and groups are fully able to carry out their functions in the community in a supportive and co-operative manner.

Again it is important to ask whether there is any resonance for these ideas within traditional African philosophy. Although all those involved with the work of the KZN-PSV have experienced this resonance, the words of African healer Malidoma Some (1998: 27) from Burkina Faso are particularly pertinent:

> There are two things that people crave: the full realisation of their innate gifts, and to have those gifts approved, acknowledged, and confirmed.

Since every community has its own particular characteristics, it is not possible to provide a comprehensive list of the different ways in which civil violence disempowers and fragments individuals, small groups, communities, and society in general. The cognitive framework presented above is suggested as a mechanism for coming to terms with the confusing and overwhelming nature of civil violence. However, some more common features of civil violence are summarised in Table 7.

This common set of effects of violence suggests a common set of empowering and linking interventions. Note that these should not be assumed to be standard to every community. It is vital that a detailed process of planning and negotiation with community structures informs particular projects. A systemic analysis of civil violence of the kind described here allows the community work to find the points of 'maximum leverage' whereby the greatest positive opportunities can be created in the community with minimum intervention and use of scarce resources. At best, the list presented in Table 8 is a list of *possibilities* around which community representatives and service providers can develop a specific intervention strategy.

Although each intervention strategy will be unique, we have found that simultaneous work on more than one aspect of the situation is most likely to produce sustainable change. The KZN-PSV strives to work with as many different people and groups in an area as possible. For example, when young men and women who had missed substantial parts of their schooling due to the civil conflict were given places on skills-training courses for employment purposes, we discovered that many became frustrated, angry, and helpless,

Table 7: Understanding civil violence in terms of fragmentation and disempowerment

	Fragmentation	Disempowerment
Individual	• Loss of memory of traumatic events. • Efforts to avoid stimuli (including thoughts) associated with traumatic events. • Cutting off one's painful feelings. • Inability to contain feelings of hopelessness, frustration, and anger. -	• Loss of control over one's life. • Inability to fulfil social roles (e.g. parent, teacher, minister, bread-winner, child). • Loss of education, training, personal development opportunities. • High stress, inability to concentrate, sleep disturbances, poor eating habits, and substance abuse impair ability to function. • Loss of interest in significant activities. • Sense of foreshortened future results in no long-term planning or vision.
Small Group	• Generalised distrust and suspicion of others. • Lack of intimacy and emotional support. • Reduced caring behaviour (parents and older siblings of small children, teachers of pupils, etc.) • Envy of friends and family. • Undermining of attempts to heal by family and friends. • Breakdown in community communication structures, leading to individual isolation (people no longer meet at church, etc.)	• Small groups unable to fulfil their roles in community (prayer groups, youth clubs, etc). • Loss of meaningful supportive, healing, and development resources within community (sports and recreation facilities, skills-training opportunities, etc.).
Community	• Destruction of valuable and scarce infrastructure and resources. • Division within community prevents resources from being optimised. • Generalised distrust of 'outsiders'. • This results in inability to access external resources or repair/ replace damaged infrastructure.	• Local structures lose their ability to represent and govern (teachers cannot enforce discipline in schools, break-away political structures form, conflict between civic and political structures emerge).

Table 7 continued

	Fragmentation	Disempowerment
	• Non-functional community structures prevent representation in local government structures (breakdown in democracy). • This results in frustration and anger and further conflict.	
Society	• Isolation of communities hinders peace-making and fosters conflict. • Increase in number of weapons in society. • Proliferation of paramilitary training.	• Intolerable strain on virtually all services, resulting in inability to function (policing, emergency services, health services, welfare services, etc.) • Development programmes constantly undermined, leading to generalised disillusionment with process of social change.

Table 8: Responding to civil violence in terms of linking and empowerment

	Linking	Empowerment

Individual	• Individual and group trauma counselling aimed at:
	  • Processing traumatic events.
	  • Learning adaptive coping techniques.
	  • Learning to contain and express emotion in controlled and adaptive manner.
		• Individual and group counselling aimed at:
		  • Understanding individual's personal narratives.
		  • Developing decision-making skills.
		  • Planning for the future.
		• Re-learning of social skills necessary to continue life in a peaceful society.
		• Opportunities for personal development.
		• Opportunities to develop self-esteem.

Small Group	• Group work aimed at building relationships:
	  • Recognising and naming ' distrust'.
	  • Exploring barriers to trust.
	  • Learning how to negotiate trusting relationships.
		• Rebuilding small groups and assisting them to fulfil their original purpose (facilitating prayer groups, youth clubs, etc.).

Table 8: continued

	Linking	Empowerment

	• Opportunities to develop intimacy and social support.
	• Developing caring behaviour.
	  • Exploring barriers to caring.
	  • Learning caring behaviour.
	• Rebuilding fragmented social structures (churches, schools, etc.).	

Community	• Rebuild infrastructure and other resources. • Peace-making and negotiation to ensure that resources are available to entire community. • Facilitate links with resources outside of communities. Empower community structures to work responsibly with outside agencies. • Facilitate the development of proper democratic local government and other community structures.	• Build the capacity of local leaders and service providers to deliver effective and accountable support to the community.
Society	• Foster links between communities, and between different levels of government. • Active lobbying against proliferation of weapons. • Active lobbying against paramilitary training.	• Support the functioning of social services (extra training and resources for police, etc.). • Support broader development and public-works programmes which offer economic relief to survivors of violence.

and that the drop-out rate was extremely high. However, when these same young people simultaneously attended a youth group that was working on issues of personal growth and interpersonal support, the drop-out rate was substantially lower. Similarly, a mothers' group which had raised funds to build a crèche was able to employ a youth group, which was being run simultaneously in the same community, to help to clean and repair the building that would house the crèche. This provided a much-needed resource for the mothers, and a manageable community project for the young people, who grew in confidence and self-esteem and were highly praised by community representatives.

Furthermore, the timing of interventions is crucial. Linking and empowerment happen at different levels at different times. This introduces a further crucial dimension, which up to this point has been missing from the model.

The time dimension

Violence disempowers and fragments at each level of society, and at different times during the process of conflict and recovery. With the above broad framework to guide us, we can begin to appreciate what needs to be achieved at each level of the community, at different times during its recovery. Different types of intervention are required, depending upon how long ago the actual violence occurred and how the community has progressed since that time. Traditional wisdom accepts that emergency relief work is the appropriate intervention immediately after an eruption of civil violence, and that capacity building, training, and other developmental work cannot be initiated until relative peace has been attained and the community's basic needs have been met. However, the work of KZN-PSV has demonstrated that such a simplistic application of interventions is not always the most beneficial – a finding which is supported by other work in similar contexts.

Roche (1996) suggests that relief and development agencies essentially participate in four categories of activity, ranging from emergency relief to long-term economic, social, and political reconstruction. He argues that all of these different activities are necessary at all times following a crisis, but that their relative importance changes. The experiences of KZN-PSV support this argument, but suggest an even more integrated conceptualisation. It is possible to ensure that a community in crisis receives the necessary shelter and food in a way that *empowers community structures* and *links the community* in a useful way, both internally and externally. Directly after a crisis, the most important linkages might well be with providers of shelter and food, and existing community structures should be empowered to negotiate access to and distribution of these resources. This is in marked contrast to the 'rescue response', which simply organises the delivery of food and tents for communities in crisis.

Once again, these comments underline the need to understand the history of each particular community, as well as the formal and informal structures of which it is composed. In this way, the community worker is able correctly to analyse the local needs at any particular time, and to assist the most appropriate internal structures to respond to those needs.

Observation of our target communities reveals that a great deal more work remains to be done on the narratives of communities exposed to civil violence. At times, communities which have survived long histories of extreme violence intact may suddenly disintegrate, with structures ceasing to function and many people moving out at once, in response to a relatively minor violent event. We do not really understand what it is that enables certain communities to weather civil violence at some points and not others. In other communities, the pattern is easier to understand. Most often people continue to support the community until the level of threat reaches a certain threshold, at which point fleeing becomes the more attractive option. In order to increase the effectiveness of our interventions, we must try to understand the factors which give people hope and provide the community with internal resilience. Similarly, we need to understand those factors that undermine resilience and result in the disintegration of the community.

The next chapter deals with some of the answers that this model of civil violence provides for the questions posed at the beginning of this chapter. In addition, it describes the process followed by the KZN-PSV in implementing community projects.

5 Plans into action: the process of intervention

A model is only as good as the extent to which it finds effective application, and is implemented in a manner which produces positive and lasting change in communities experiencing civil violence.

On which communities should attention and resources be focused?

Owing to the pervasiveness of the civil violence, it was necessary to target particular communities (defined geographically). The map of KwaZulu-Natal in Chapter 2 shows the two centres from which the KZN-PSV operates, as well as the communities targeted over the past several years. These include both urban and rural communities, as well as informal settlements. Virtually every one of these communities has experienced at least one resurgence of violent civil conflict between 1994 and the present. They have very few health-care, social-welfare, or education services, and are characterised by a lack of infrastructure and high unemployment and crime levels. They exhibit a broad range of social problems, including teenage pregnancy, HIV infection, and abuse of alcohol and other substances.

Thus, the process of intervention starts with decisions about how best to allocate resources. This debate centres on two questions:

- How should resources be distributed? Or, how many different communities of what size can we work with effectively?
- To which communities should resources be allocated?

The answer to the first question depends largely upon the resources available, of course. More financial resources, more equipment (particularly vehicles), and more personnel make it possible to replicate the process in more communities. At the beginning of the project's life, we started work in two communities only. Today, the project is working in approximately fifteen areas simultaneously.

A more useful approach is to consider what level of resources is necessary in order to be effective in a particular community. In order to make any lasting change, we have discovered that it is necessary to run at least two simultaneous and complementary interventions (for example, work with local leadership and militarised youth, or with mothers and children). In order to run a single intervention, community workers must be able to visit the target area at least twice per week. Given these rough figures, it is possible to work out how many areas the agency is equipped to work in, at any given time.

Once the capacity of the agency has been determined in this manner, it becomes possible to start the complex and painful process of choosing which communities to work with. This is helped a great deal by applying initial selection criteria. Target communities should have explicitly expressed their desire for assistance from the agency. In other words, decision makers should be choosing from a range of requests for work, rather than merely from a list of communities that are considered to be in need. Four other criteria are also used by the KZN-PSV.

- It targets those communities that have experienced the worst levels of civil violence.

- It considers that a reasonable level of security, which will allow field workers to assist in the area without endangering themselves, is important. Where communities are extremely volatile, security measures are required before useful developmental work can be attempted.

- KZN-PSV works in those areas that can be readily accessed from one of its centres. This ensures maximal benefit from limited resources, since travel is costly in terms of finances and staff time.

- The organisation ensures that equal resources are allocated to communities aligned to the various warring parties in the region. If this is not ensured, it is very easy for support agencies unwittingly to compound the tensions.

Being able to state these criteria explicitly enables the organisation to justify difficult choices to its own staff, to community leaders whose requests cannot be met, and to other stakeholders.

When target communities have been established, it becomes possible to begin the community-intervention process. The most appropriate staff within the organisation are selected to work in that community, and the necessary internal support and supervision structures are established. These community workers are then required to become familiar with the detailed history and internal dynamics of the community, before beginning the negotiation and planning processes.

What intervention strategy is best suited to a particular community?

Determining the content of an intervention within a selected target community is a process of careful negotiation and planning with local community leaders and opinion-formers.

Negotiation and planning

Negotiation begins with whichever community structure made the request for assistance. Very often such requests come from local leaders, but requests have also been received through political party offices, youth organisations, and women's groups. It is virtually always necessary to broaden out the initial group, to obviate the danger of an 'accountability gap' and to mobilise as many resources within the community as possible. An 'accountability gap' emerges when a particular group within a community claims to represent the interests of the entire community, in most cases with honourable intentions. For example, many communities in KwaZulu-Natal have development committees which strongly argue that issues such as housing, water supply, and employment are the most important concerns of local people. However, a more detailed analysis of the lives of working women in the community often reveals that health-care and child-care facilities are their major concern. In order to build a strong foundation for a community project, the community workers should facilitate a process by which all the competing concerns can be voiced. This involves building a broader project team, which incorporates all kinds of people within the community, so as to cover the broadest range of concerns and available resources.

During this process, community representatives discuss various priorities and ideas for effective community intervention. Agency representatives facilitate the process and offer suggestions, based upon their experience in other communities and their knowledge of developmental social work. A danger at this point is that local people begin to feel overwhelmed by the challenges that their community faces and so lose interest or energy. Community workers must be able to assist local leaders to make sense of the problems in a way which does not discourage them.

Through this process, a strategic plan is developed for work within the community which is designed to link and empower, thereby reversing the fragmentary and disempowering effects of civil violence. Clearly, the strategic plan for any community will depend to a great extent on the current situation, the history, the resources, and the concerns of people within the community. The choice of a particular intervention also depends upon knowing what resources the community has to work with. It is essential for the project team to make the greatest possible use of all available resources, and for community workers to acquire a deep understanding of the history, geography, and social dynamics of the target area. During the negotiation phase of intervention, community workers must make community profiling one of their highest priorities.

Community profiling

During this phase the community worker is engaged in many activities.

- **Learning the history of the community, as understood by community members.** This history is contained within the numerous (and often contradictory) stories and anecdotes about the area which are told by adults in the community. The history of Bhambayi (see Box overleaf), as told by members of the community, illustrates this clearly. Although it may be difficult to piece together a single, authenticated, and coherent history for a community, it is the multiple stories and beliefs which are important. How people understand their own situation must be the basis for the rebuilding of their lives.

- **Understanding the leadership structures, both formal and informal, in the area.** In many of KwaZulu-Natal's communities it is local party-political leaders who have great influence, whereas the official local councils, development committees, and recognised traditional leadership may in fact have less power.

- **Developing an understanding of the internal and external resources available to the community.** These resources include everything from a monthly visit of a mobile primary health-care unit, to a teacher in the local school who has training in child care, to the fact that a senior provincial or national politician comes from the community and might be willing to become involved in work in his or her home town.

- **Developing an understanding of the social dynamics that might sabotage work in the community.** Such dynamics could take the form of a local leader in opposition who stands to benefit from discrediting the work, or the fact that the local police support a particular interest-group within the community.

Only with a deep understanding of the community's functioning can the appropriate strategic intervention be undertaken.

Box 1: Bhambayi and its multiple histories

There are several interesting stories about the origins of the warfare in Bhambayi. One relates the move of people displaced by violence in northern and southern parts of KwaZulu, and from the Eastern Cape (the province to the south of KwaZulu-Natal) into the area called 'Bombay'. The people describe how nearly thirty years ago the local Indian population were forced out of the community and their homes taken from them. The ruins of older homes belonging to people with more resources do stand everywhere in Bhambayi today.

A second story goes that there was a traditional healer who was appointed to look after the community, and each household had to pay a monthly fee to this healer for protection. However, people became unhappy when he raised the fee to R 60 per family. Some started supporting another leader, closer to them, who was charging only R 30 per family. This caused great tension, and some say that a curse was put on the area. Others say that the tension did involve these two leaders, but that the cause of the tension was not financial, but ethnic. People chose to give their allegiance to the healer who came from their own area of origin, and in fact the fighting in Bhambayi was a continuation of an older conflict.

Eventually and predictably, the division of Bhambayi was exploited by political movements in the area. When one side reportedly went to the ANC for armed support, the other side claimed that they were forced to join the IFP for support. With the community's youth armed and trained by the political players, the fighting continued in the area for more than ten years.

Project implementation

It is important to note that intervention is unlikely to be of short duration. In order to achieve real and lasting change at the community level, years of intensive work are required. The social fabric of a community may be destroyed in a few short weeks of intense conflict, but may take a decade or more to rebuild. One-off high-profile interventions, such as training a group of lay trauma-counsellors, or training mothers to operate a crèche, are popular with both agencies and donors. It is our experience, however, that without the fundamental work of linking and empowering, such interventions have little or no lasting effect upon community life.

For this reason, starting work in a new community is an extremely serious undertaking, because it commits the organisation to work there for the foreseeable future. Furthermore, if the agency starts to get results, it is likely that more and more projects will be required, not fewer and fewer. Thus, as time passes, the commitment of resources to target communities increases rather than decreases. If the work proceeds smoothly, it is likely that the agency will be required to work with differing groups within the same community and in differing ways. Thus, a support group established for ex-combatant youths is likely to grow into training programmes and job-creation projects for them. This in turn is likely to prompt other young people in the community to ask for assistance in developing their own skills. In other cases, adults in the community may see the success that the young people are having and wish to start projects which address the needs of adults or children. In this way the work grows and links up with other initiatives, and a comprehensive response to the challenges facing the community starts to emerge.

What the actual implementation phase within a particular community will consist of cannot be described, because it will be different for every community. The following chapters describe some of the ways in which the KZN-PSV has worked in order to facilitate the recovery of some communities in KwaZulu-Natal.

How to prevent burn-out and secondary traumatic stress among field staff?

When a community worker starts work in a particular area, she or he becomes part of the complex dynamics within that community. The dynamics of fragmentation and disempowerment apply just as strongly to the community workers as they do to the local population, and they must constantly struggle towards the goals of linking and empowerment. For example, the act of entering a community often leaves community workers feeling overwhelmed by the difficulties (disempowered) and with a sense that their families and friends cannot understand the tremendous strain of the work (fragmented).

Thus the model suggests multiple ways of assisting staff and thus preventing burn-out. First, a clear strategy is crucial. Having a plan is one of the best ways to combat feelings of being disempowered. Consider again the community workers described at the beginning of the previous chapter. Had they entered the community with a plan to establish a crèche to assist working mothers in the community, thus enabling children to play safely and mothers to work with less fear for their children's safety (empowerment) – a crèche which would be run by unemployed mothers in the community for an affordable fee (empowerment), and which would serve as a site for a new children's health project to be run by the mobile clinic (linking) – the workers would not have felt so overwhelmed by the problems facing a single family. They would be less likely to burn out and much more likely to bring lasting change to the community.

Second, proper training is important, and on-going staff development is necessary – not only to build the organisation, but to make community workers feel that they are competent to deal with the challenges of their work. Third, and most important, is the need to work on relationships and social support, both within the organisation and community workers' personal lives. More advice on stress and burn-out is included in the final chapter.

What limits should be set on the involvement with a particular community?

Limiting the organisation's commitment to a particular community depends upon accurate information regarding the impact of existing work on the community, and how well the community is functioning at any particular time. This depends upon the process of monitoring and evaluation.

Monitoring and evaluation

As community dynamics change, the intervention strategies of community agencies must change too. For example, if it happens after three years of working in a community that a multinational corporation decides to erect a factory in the area, employment-skills training of young people in the area must be modified to meet the needs of the factory.

The linking and empowerment model suggests a range of more appropriate markers or indicators upon which monitoring and evaluation work may be based. For example, instead of measuring the number of violent deaths in a community per month (which is dependent on multiple factors, many unrelated to the health of the community), it might be better to measure the number of external service agencies that local leaders have managed to draw into the community (an indicator of the linking capacity of the community). If local leaders manage to organise a permanent clinic in the community, that is a very positive sign of sustainable development and community health. Similarly, the number of churches operating, or the number of teachers working in a community, better represents the health and resilience of an area than the level of fighting or number of deaths, which are more traditionally used as indicators in this field.

An action-research paradigm is the appropriate tool for this type of monitoring and evaluation. It is vital for community and agency representatives to review their work on a regular basis, in order to maximise the impact of the agreed intervention. This process of continuous reflection, self-critique, and adjustment is crucial for effective intervention in unstable and fragmented communities. As communities change, so must the extent and nature of the projects run by supportive agencies such as the KZN-PSV. The following chapters describe a range of projects run by the organisation over the past ten years. They are organised in terms of various population groups within communities, but this structure is somewhat misleading, as it tends to suggest that the work with young people, for example, is divorced from the work with community leadership or with women. This is not that case. At all times, projects are designed to be complementary and mutually supportive. The greater aim is to bring lasting change to the community, and not merely to address the concerns of particular groups within it.

One important indicator that the time is right to bring to a close the organisation's work within a particular community is when the community demonstrates the capacity to resolve internal conflicts peacefully, and to resolve other challenges facing its members without external assistance.

6 Work with young people

'We are carrying out the revenge for our parents. It is time for us to work out how to stop this cycle, because it is ruining our lives.' (Youth-group member)

Young people have been prioritised by the staff and board of the KZN-PSV since the organisation's earliest days. For this reason, school children were the focus of the research work described in Chapter 3. However, we quickly discovered that, despite the alarming levels of distress within the population of school children, it was rather the young people who had left the education system to participate in the civil violence in their communities who were most in need of assistance.

Sadly, the greatest perpetrators and victims of violence in KwaZulu-Natal are young people who left school as a result of their involvement in the struggle against apartheid rule, and subsequently became caught up in the civil conflict. This is true of both young men and young women, but in different ways. The highly patriarchal structure of Zulu society meant that very few women were trained for combat within the paramilitary structures of the ANC and IFP. While older boys and young men left school in order to become combatants, many older girls were entrusted with the care of younger siblings and cousins. In these cases they were often sent to stay with relatives in safer communities, which once again disrupted the usual activities of adolescent life in the community, including attendance at school. Being forced to leave their homes in this way and being entrusted with young children in a war situation imposed on young women their own particular set of stresses, which are the subject of a later chapter.

The following account by TM, a 21-year-old male member of a youth group in KwaMashu, illustrates the experience of young people in the area.

❧ Violence affected me and my fellow youth, as the community is now divided. Those who have an education look down on youth who did not get one. There is a great deal of tension between these two groups. The SAP [South African Police] had a hand in violence, and this resulted in me having a deep hatred of the police. Violence also resulted in us losing our education, losing our relationship with our parents, and I have to take part in some activities which are illegal. But I need the money. I need some sort of way to make a living. I see people who have something and I envy them, and the only way to get it, to get where they are, is the illegal way. Envy and hatred is always a part of me. I know it's no use to cry over spoilt milk, over a mad situation, no use to fight to get what you want. **❜**

This testimony raises a number of themes which are central to work with young people following civil conflict. They include questions of self-esteem (feeling despised by educated people), anger and hatred (directed at the police and others in the community), loss of support and intimacy (including relationships with parents), threats to mental health (*'envy and hatred are always a part of me'*), the need to build an adult life (family, home, employment issues), and involvement in crime and violence. However, it is a mistake to imagine that the worst experiences of young people are those of direct civil conflict. Experiences resulting from the destruction of social life within the community may be equally disruptive. The following quotations, collected from young men and women in our groups, illustrate the diversity of ways in which young people's lives have been adversely affected.

Figure 8 ANC youths, using a military vehicle as cover, throw stones at the houses of Inkatha supporters, June 1995.

- 'Sifiso organised a meeting in a church that was surrounded by the police: the police didn't want to listen and started shooting, people ran and some were shot, some were run over by cars. As the person who organised the meeting, he feels to blame.'

- 'His brother was killed by police, and Mvume really wanted revenge, but friends talked him out of it.'

- 'Thuli witnessed a fight between a girlfriend and boyfriend. The boy shot the girl dead at close range. She couldn't tell anyone what she saw, because she was scared.'

- 'Residents from another section came over the hill and fired on Eugene's family, burning houses and driving them away. They had to run to the Indian area.'

- 'The other party tried to drive out the youth. Solly and his friends had to live in the canefield for three months.'

- 'The chief told them to leave the area. Lungile's father was killed; now she and her family have no home.'

- 'The mother of one of them visited to talk to her son. She was killed when she went home. Now no-one feels safe to contact their families.'

- 'He witnessed two friends killing each other because of political affiliation. They were good friends before.'

- 'He witnessed a man being burned by the necklace method [tyre filled with petrol put around a person's neck and set alight]. The mob was angry because of the man's action against the community, but it was so cruel to see someone die that way.'

This broad range of unhappy experiences relates to the destruction of the supportive social fabric so vital to adolescent development. This destruction was perpetrated first by colonists, then by apartheid racism (particularly through education policies), then by the violence of the struggle to overthrow the apartheid regime, and finally by the civil conflict for control of KwaZulu-Natal. Today gang-related violence and organised crime compound the problems.

The KZN-PSV has found that in KwaZulu-Natal work with youth in small groups is most effective. The fundamental reason for this is that many young people have already been organised into small groups of paramilitary bands, and more recently criminal gangs. Although in the beginning the youth groups run by the organisation consisted mainly of young men, this pattern is changing, and some of the current groups are dominated by young women. These groups serve to confirm members' sense of identity and give them a sense of belonging and support – functions which in other societies are fulfilled by sports teams, the family, the school, and so on.

Many agencies working with militarised youth aim to demobilise and disarm combatants. In the experience of the KZN-PSV, this approach runs the risk of destroying the agency's credibility within a community which relies on armed youth for protection, and it is not effective in reducing the level of violence. Demobilising armed youth involves breaking down their paramilitary structures, thus taking away participants' sense of belonging, their identity, and opportunities to demonstrate their abilities and be respected by their peers. Instead the KZN-PSV specifically targets paramilitary units, gangs, and the young men in control of these structures, encouraging them to join alternative and more constructive activities.

Setting up and running youth groups

It is necessary and appropriate that youth groups are run on a 'open' basis. In other words, people are free to enter and leave a group as they like. It is acceptable to attend one or two group meetings in order to test the waters, and to bring friends to the group meeting. 'Closed' groups, whose members agree to work together for a set period of time and not join or leave the process in the middle, are exclusive, in that some people will always be prevented from becoming members. When this happens in a highly suspicious and fragmented community, the potential for further conflict is increased, and community workers rapidly lose the trust of the people they are working with. It is common for youth groups in these communities to be closely monitored, and for a couple of young people closely linked to the political leadership in the area to attend on an irregular basis.

The prevailing high levels of suspicion and caution mean that the work of youth groups can quite easily be misinterpreted or misunderstood. This has happened to the KZN-PSV on more than one occasion and is potentially extremely hazardous to the work of the organisation, the community workers, and most particularly to the youth-group members themselves. For this reason it is essential that community leaders are kept informed about and involved in the work of the youth groups. Difficulties arise when leaders begin to feel threatened or undermined. With regular contact between community workers and community leadership, this threat can be managed in such a way that the leadership's monitoring of the youth groups becomes supportive, rather than controlling and suspicious.

The activities of a youth group in Greytown in 1996 illustrate these dangers clearly. At the time, the Zulu population of a township in Greytown was severely divided between supporters of the ANC and the IFP. There were frequent violent clashes between youth from these two sides. The KZN-PSV was running youth groups simultaneously on both sides of the conflict and working hard to reduce the level of violence in the area. Through the work done in the groups, the young people on the IFP side decided spontaneously, and without informing the community workers, to set up a meeting with the opposing youth to try to bring an end to the cycle of revenge killings that had been going on. This extremely dangerous meeting took place on neutral territory, but resulted in the young people on the IFP side being branded as 'sell-outs' by the IFP leadership in the community. As a result their lives were in grave danger, and it was only through extremely prompt action and difficult meetings between the community workers and the local political leadership that further killing was averted. It will be appreciated that youth work is potentially extremely hazardous in situations of civil violence. It must be undertaken in close collaboration with local political leadership, and transparency and fairness must be strictly maintained at all times.

Group meetings are run by the KZN-PSV on a weekly basis for the most part. One of the core functions of the group is to provide some kind of structure within the typically chaotic lives of the participants. Thus the groups are run at the same time, on the same day of the week, in the same venue, and according to the same basic protocols every time. This is an important step for young people towards taking control of their lives.

Composition of the youth groups

The youth groups run by the KZN-PSV have until very recently been unilateral in composition. In other words, in a fragmented community with young people's allegiance divided between the ANC and IFP, the organisation would run two groups in parallel, one for each side of the conflict. In more recent years, some communities have taken substantial steps towards lasting peace, so that the opportunities for joint youth work are becoming more and more frequent, and the first bilateral groups have been formed. Nevertheless, there remain many challenges in integrating supporters of the ANC and IFP, in part due to other differences between these two groups of young people. The political ideologies and recruitment strategies of the two political organisations have resulted in two distinct groups: supporters of the ANC tend to be more articulate, used to being able to express their opinions and grievances, and less respectful of traditional culture and their elders. Young people on the IFP side of the conflict tend to have greater respect for their elders and tradition, and are unused to expressing themselves in a group. The danger inherent in this division is that IFP supporters feel unable to interact with the youth group. Unless properly facilitated, the experience can become *disempowering* and may further isolate these young men and women.

The gender composition of groups is also important. The ambition of the KZN-PSV has always been to ensure that all youth groups consist of equal numbers of women and men. Sadly, this has never been achieved, and most youth groups have been dominated by males, with females comprising between 25 per cent and 30 per cent of the membership.

Ownership

Everything about the youth groups is aimed at *empowering* the participants, and providing opportunities for useful *linking* with resources within themselves, their communities, and the broader society. Most importantly, ownership of the group lies with its members and not with the community worker from KZN-PSV, or any other structure within the community. Where many members of the group are from a particular paramilitary organisation or other community structure, this might need to be very carefully negotiated. If the process is going to achieve its goals of empowerment, young people themselves must be completely in control of the structure.

Thus it is important for the group to decide upon a name for itself, elect its own office bearers, establish agendas for each meeting, develop its own rules and norms of behaviour, develop policies for action when those norms are not adhered to, and administer all other aspects of its own functioning. Thus, for example, one early group decided to name themselves Zamani (*We Endeavour!*); they held elections for a chairperson, secretary, and treasurer, and laid down rules for how group members should behave. These rules included a requirement to attend every meeting of the group, or in special circumstances send an apology and explanation for one's absence. The tasks of cleaning the venue before and after meetings and preparing a light lunch were distributed equally among all group members (male and female). Lateness was punishable with a fine, which was added to the group's savings for use on projects and training courses and so forth.

Most important to young people's ownership of their own structures is the question of finances. Youth groups can generate funds in multiple ways, including donations from people in the community, subscription fees and fines paid by members, and the proceeds of community projects such as film shows, for which entrance can be charged, or selling chickens. Finally, some donor agencies have made donations directly to youth groups. Administering finances is somewhat difficult. Banks require a clear constitution, formal practices of accounting, and so forth before they will allow an account to be opened. This is very difficult for new youth groups to deal with, so until they are properly constituted, funds are managed through the KZN-PSV. The treasurer of the group, together with the group facilitator, is responsible for keeping a set of accounts to show how much money belonging to the group is lodged with the KZN-PSV. In this way group members learn about managing finances, budgeting, bank accounts, and so on.

Of course, not all young people have the capacity to manage a youth group in this way, especially when many of the members are illiterate and deeply traumatised by their experiences of civil conflict. Managing a basic savings account for the group may be very challenging, and where there is a concern about how money is being spent, the resulting conflict can quickly destroy the group and even lead to physical violence. Many of these young people carry deep anger at their situation in life; they are very suspicious and easily frustrated. This, combined with the fact that they are often also armed, produces a potentially dangerous state of affairs.

A great deal of the work in youth groups is thus invested in building the group's capacity to manage itself. In so doing, of course, the members of the group are learning valuable skills for managing themselves in the broader environment as well. When problems arise within the group, it is vital that the community worker should identify the problem early, bring it to the group's attention, and help the members to deal with it in a way which teaches them about skilful conflict management without disempowering them.

Content of the group sessions

In line with the above, the members themselves determine the content of group sessions. Sessions deal with the challenges of adolescence, both those encountered in a more stable and safe society and the problems of reaching adulthood in a society experiencing or recovering from civil conflict. Some important and common areas of work are described below.

Managing feelings

It is common for adolescents to struggle with managing their own feelings. These struggles are magnified by the experiences of betrayal, exploitation, loss, and victimisation that are part of civil conflict. Many of the young people in our groups are filled with sadness, rage, frustration, jealousy, and hopelessness. For the most part these feelings remain hidden, but they surface repeatedly to sabotage personal progress. Learning how to recognise and express these feelings safely and in an appropriate way is an important learning experience. One member testified:

> ❪ I came to this workshop a very shy person, carrying a lot of helplessness and hopelessness, but I feel I was being heard and taken seriously by other participants in the group. I felt I was ready to pursue a new life. ❫

Negotiating relationships

Adolescence is also a time of negotiating and renegotiating relationships with peers, possible love partners, parents, potential employers, and other people within the community. When young people are burdened with all the destructive feelings outlined above, the business of building relationships becomes extremely arduous. Furthermore, having spent many adolescent years within paramilitary structures or on the run, young people have often not had opportunities to develop these important life skills. When all strangers are regarded as potential threats, one does not learn how to start and sustain a conversation, express one's feelings honestly but responsibly, trust others and be trustworthy, give and receive constructive feedback, and so forth.

Many young people in our groups fail to build the relationships necessary for their lives to progress in a healthy fashion. The group provides formal and informal learning opportunities. Formal group sessions often include discussions on themes such as '*Boys like ... and girls like*', which is about how to form relationships with people of the opposite sex, and '*My parents don't understand that ...*', which deals with inter-generational relationship building, assertiveness training, and so forth. Informally, the groups put young people in a situation where they cannot help but build relationships with strangers (including group facilitators), other members of the group, and through youth projects with other people within their community and beyond it.

It is vitally important for young people to develop confidence in their ability to build relationships. This confidence comes from repeated success in overcoming challenges and being recognised for that by others. Youth workers are on hand to try to ensure that young people do successfully negotiate relationships, and to help them recognise this when they do. Of course, this means working with some very difficult and stressful interpersonal dynamics, as youth members struggle to relate effectively. It is most important during this time that young people do not fail in their relationship-building attempts. While success and praise build a sense of self-confidence, failure reinforces the sense of hopelessness and helplessness.

The benefit of work on managing feelings and negotiating relationships became apparent in an unexpected way. One of the ways in which youth groups assist young people is by helping them to identify opportunities to develop skills which will enable them to generate their own income. Thus, many young men and women attend youth groups and employment-skills training courses simultaneously. These courses are run by other agencies which specialise in such work and are linked to the KZN-PSV. Two chronic problems faced by employment-skills training agencies is that a high number of trainees drop out from their courses, or, having completed their courses, are soon dismissed from their new jobs. An evaluation of the training agency's work demonstrated that young men and women who were also involved in KZN-PSV's groups were better able to contain their frustrations and anger on the training courses and in their first jobs. In addition, they were better able to develop constructive relationships with trainers and employers and to resolve problems before those problems led to their dropping out of the course, or being dismissed from work.

Personal development and culture

Many young people are troubled by distress that originates in their life histories or current positions. Although this distress is often easily comparable with anxiety disorders (such as post-traumatic and acute stress disorders) and mood disorders (most commonly various forms of depression), it is unhelpful in the vast majority of cases to offer any kind of diagnosis to youth-group members. Where mental-health services are virtually non-existent, little is gained from adding a stigmatising label to existing problems.

As an alternative, the youth group can be a positive force for mental health. Firstly, the group provides a vehicle for emotional expression among peers and emotional support from them. In a sense, the group provides the setting for the 'exposing to view' rituals described in Chapter 3. Secondly, the group provides a forum for talking about alternative ways of coping. Young people develop many strategies to cope with the pain of their past experiences and the reality of their current situations. Some are effective, and others are ultimately destructive. In group sessions we talk about effective coping and share ideas and strategies. Thirdly, the group allows for learning about emotional and mental health in a way that equips people to manage their own problems better. For example, some of the symptoms of traumatic stress, such as flash-backs, are associated in the popular perception with psychosis, or 'madness'. Discussions of what flashbacks are and why people experience them increase the possibility of control, and are thus empowering. One group participant had this to say about his mental health and the support of his group:

> ❟ I get upset easily, I do not trust any one and have no confidence in myself. Emotionally, I'm upside down ... In the group I learn that I am not alone in such a situation. When I am alone I am self-blaming, self-hating, but as part of the group I can see a way forward. ❟

Finally, the group provides an opportunity for young people to access individual counselling for themselves and the broader circle of people within the community with whom they interact. The KZN-PSV employs two people whose main activity in the organisation is helping people who for whatever reasons cannot be assisted in groups run within the community.

Consideration of the mental-health aspect of the youth-group activities raises again the issue (previously discussed in Chapter 3) of whether core concepts of mental health which are 'Western' in origin are applicable within an African (predominantly Zulu) context. Adolescents, more than any other members of South African society, are caught between the diverse cultures of their country. Their childhoods were often rooted firmly in African traditional culture, but as they grow up they are exposed, through education, the media, and personal contact, to the 'merchandising' of the West and its values and aspirations; they are also exposed to the rival claims of political parties, struggling either to revive traditional rule or to promote a multi-party democracy. These young people are expected to value simultaneously the traditional African coming-of-age ceremonies, fashionable 'designer' jeans, and the right to freedom of speech. These examples illustrate the deep divisions in ideology and loyalty with which many young people in South Africa are obliged to contend. Naturally the assumption that their needs and concerns are identical to those of Western adolescents is false. But the assumption that they are wholly African is equally misleading. At best, the experience of these young people is multi-cultural; at worst, it is a-cultural. All must grapple with the complex, often painful, and ultimately personal issues of identity, loyalty, and belief. In the words of a member of the KZN-PSV staff:

> ❟ The youth are carrying so much. I always forget how much they have been through, and each time I hear the stories, I am shocked all over again. ❟

Skills training

Youth groups also include a range of skills-development activities, within three broad categories. The first relates to personal skills (of which negotiating relationships has already been singled out). Other personal skills include language skills, personal presentation, decision-making, stress management, and time management. Language is important, because these young people have missed out on developing their command of the English language. Good spoken English is a very important skill for finding employment in KwaZulu-Natal. Because youth do not have many opportunities to practise their English with fluent speakers, they sometimes ask for group sessions to be conducted in English.

The second category of skills involves actual training for employment. Many young people are lacking in skills, due to the early disruption of their education. They need opportunities to develop skills to make them more employable. Without reasonable possibilities of earning an income and supporting themselves, it is virtually impossible for these men and women to

Paul Weinberg/KZN PSV/Oxfam

Figure 9 Bongiwe, aged 28, displays juggling skills learned with the African Dream Circus, a project facilitated by KZN-PSV and Cirque du Soleil, which engages in community arts projects.

make progress in their lives. The KZN-PSV does not have the technical or personnel capacity to offer employment-skills training directly; so it works in partnership with a range of other structures (mostly non-government agencies) which do offer training in a wide variety of work skills, including brick-laying, plumbing, electrical installation and repair work, tiling, painting, metal work, secretarial work, and computer skills. Acquiring these skills takes an enormous amount of commitment and concentration on the part of young people who have not participated in formal education for several years and are struggling with the emotional burden that results from years of exposure to civil conflict. The drop-out rates are high – and, even for those who do complete the training, the current employment situation in KwaZulu-Natal (and indeed in South Africa generally) is extremely problematic and seemingly getting worse. However, with support and encouragement, young men and women who have completed their training do find odd jobs which they use to demonstrate their ability, then they get short-contract work, and eventually end up in full-time employment. It is a bitter struggle to become economically self-sufficient, and the staff of the KZN-PSV work hard to make young people aware of this from the very beginning. Young people must not be led to believe that if they attend a certain training course then they will easily find a job and earn an income, and that their life circumstances will improve swiftly. In reality this is extremely unlikely, and when, after investing an enormous amount of effort under difficult circumstances, the young person's expectations are not met, the feelings of betrayal and helplessness undermine any positive progress that he or she has made.

Young women often find themselves in a particularly difficult position with regard to acquiring employment skills. Zulu communities do not encourage women to search for jobs. 'Women's work' is clearly defined and is largely restricted to household duties, child rearing, and subsistence farming. For this reason relatively few young women seek out job skills and employment for themselves. Those who do so find themselves with fewer opportunities than their male counterparts, since the training agencies tend to focus largely on construction-type work, and the women trainees end up competing for work in an environment where employers favour men. In addition, these young women find themselves in opposition to their parents, elders, and community leaders. In these cases their only support comes from the other young men and women in the youth group, and the group's facilitators.

The third category of skills training involves those skills required to plan and implement community projects. As noted above, these young people are not in school and are not working, and so there exist few opportunities (with the exception of those on the battlefield) to demonstrate competence and ability. In order for people in this position to develop self-esteem, they must be involved in something constructive. For this reason the staff of the KZN-PSV involve young people in community projects of their own choosing and design. Such projects have included raising poultry and making blocks for building houses, as well as organising talent and beauty contests, film shows, and other events for young people in their community. Where possible these projects generate enough income to send group members on work-skills training courses, and to meet other expenses that the group might incur.

In addition, youth projects allow young people to develop a wider range of life skills, including planning skills, fund-raising and budgeting, and public speaking. One project that has involved many young people and offered a sustainable service to the community is the peer-counselling project, with participants from various groups in several areas. In this project, interested young people are trained to support and assist other young people in their communities. This training is conducted by the staff of KZN-PSV directly, since the necessary technical expertise is available within the organisation. The following is an outline of the peer-counselling training programme:

- *Introduction and Rationale for the Course:* During this session, participants are challenged to explore their reasons for volunteering and their expectations of the project. The group also establishes its own norms of behaviour, including issues of confidentiality and contracting.

- *Understanding Ourselves as Peer-Support Workers:* Participants explore their own histories and life stories. This exercise is used to identify commonalities and build support within the group.

- *Understanding and Dealing with Stress and Trauma:* In this session trainees use their own experiences to learn about stress and traumatic stress and how to provide useful support and information to other young people struggling to come to terms with traumatic experiences.

- *Stress and Trauma Counselling:* At this point in the training programme, participants are provided with a basic trauma-counselling model, based on controlled re-exposure to the traumatic event, cognitive reframing (examining the experience from various perspectives, in order to understand it more deeply and realistically), and developing adaptive coping mechanisms and social support.

- *Self-esteem Building:* Work on self-esteem is critical to youth work. Participants are challenged to examine their own self-image and to analyse the processes that inform that image. In particular, participants are asked to identify their own strengths and weaknesses.

- *Human Behaviour and the Social Environment:* During this session participants are introduced to ways of understanding people holistically. This involves considering a person as a whole entity: body, thoughts, feelings, relationships with family and friends, home, culture, spiritual beliefs, history, and so on.

- *Decision Making and Problem Solving:* In this session participants analyse decision-making processes, to enable them to assist others in making difficult choices.

Once this broad range of skills has been mastered, the peer-counsellors continue to meet on a weekly basis for support and supervision. During these sessions they continue their training, on self-selected topics including assertiveness; adolescence and early adulthood; human anatomy; HIV and AIDS; substance abuse; gangsterism; Satanism; gender roles; human rights; sexual, physical, and emotional abuse; depression; and suicide.

Helping youth to gain a sense of control over their difficult histories and current circumstances is the longest-established type of work in KZN-PSV. Its value is demonstrated in these words from a parent of a member of one of the youth groups:

> ❝ Whatever medicine you have given my son this past week, please don't stop. He is a totally different person. ❞

Work with youth gangs: a special group

The changing face of the political conflict in KwaZulu-Natal, together with the gaps in many people's education and training, and the high levels of unemployment in the area, has made crime and gangsterism an attractive alternative for many young people. Gangs pose a growing threat to communities in the area, and it has become imperative that the programme start to address this problem. The dynamics of gangs are very different from those of the quasi-military units of political conflict, and once again we had to begin work with a lengthy and frustrating process of trying to understand gangs before we could do anything very useful to combat their negative effects upon individuals, families, and the community.

Understanding gangs

Within the province there is a growing acknowledgement of the large numbers of young men who are becoming involved in crime. The policy of the government has at times been fairly tough, demanding a reduction in criminal activities of youth and gangs through more stringent security, policing, and judicial interventions. This kind of response, which makes no attempt to understand the reasons why young people become involved in gangs, is only ever likely to address the symptoms of the problem, not its causes. While necessary in order to protect citizens and their property, such a response is very limited. Some deeper form of research to understand gang dynamics was felt to be necessary.

The KZN-PSV and its partners embarked on a multi-method research project, upon which an intervention designed to combat the proliferation of gangs might be based. This research began with the development of a database relating to young people involved in crime and gangs. Data were collected by means of a detailed questionnaire, designed to obtain information on the following broad themes:

- Factors promoting involvement in violent crime.
- Factors discouraging involvement in violent crime.
- Social identity, role models, and sense of belonging.
- Benefits of involvement in criminal gangs.
- Disadvantages of involvement in criminal gangs.

One of the major challenges of the questionnaire was to encourage honest responses without fear of repercussions, so a lengthy introduction was added to the questionnaire, guaranteeing anonymity and confidentiality. A second consideration was the need to prevent the respondents feeling discouraged or hopeless following reflection on their answers, since many of the questions were quite personal and required the respondent to think more deeply about his or her choices. The questionnaire thus ended with questions about the person's hopes and dreams, and an invitation to contact the staff members of the organisation for further assistance.

To compensate for the difficulties inherent in collecting data by means of questionnaires, focus-group discussions were also conducted. They enabled the researchers to cross-validate the findings of two studies and to access a broader range of information. Focus-group discussions were conducted with the young people who were already involved in work with the KZN-PSV. The trust built up in the programme's on-going youth work provided the necessary foundation for the difficult conversations about involvement in crime and gangs. Most particularly the work on traumatic stress was very useful in this regard. This work provides young people with an opportunity to tell the stories of their lives, to understand their personal history, their current state and feelings about their lives, and their sense of social identity, and to formulate their plans for the future. The focus groups also provided an opportunity to test some of the emerging hypotheses relating to intervention strategies.

Finally, a third method of individual interviews and case studies was included, in order to deeper our understanding of young people's involvement in gangs. Unstructured interviews were conducted with young people who were prepared to speak honestly and in detail about their life experiences pertaining to involvement in crime and gangs. The most striking result was that most of the young people who got involved in crime and especially gangs reported doing so as a direct consequence of their own traumatic experiences. Respondents described their sense of alienation from others, and their sense of being misunderstood and being social misfits. They also described giving violent expression to the anger that they felt about their experiences. This is a highly significant result, given the multiple and severe exposure to trauma faced by so many young men and women in KwaZulu-Natal. Further investigation would be useful in determining the age of their exposure to trauma, and other mediating factors. It is also important to note that many of the young people who chose *not* to be involved in violence had also been exposed to traumatic experiences: the additional mediating factors require careful analysis.

It emerges that those young people reporting excessive amounts of unresolved anger are particularly at risk of becoming involved in crime and gangs. The following quotation clearly illustrates this relationship.

> ❢ I saw my sister being raped by a gang, right in front of me. I have never forgotten this image, although we never spoke about it again. I watched as my sister became more and more withdrawn, eventually hardly leaving the house. This made me so angry, and I vowed to revenge. I did not feel able to do this alone, and formed a group of young men willing to assist me. I trained them in fighting skills, and also how to dress and to speak so as to fit in a township setting. ❧

The links between violence, gangs, anger, and the urge to take revenge have emerged consistently throughout the research and are particularly strong when young people have experienced or witnessed offences for which the perpetrators have not been punished and the victims have not been compensated. Under these circumstances, victims feel the need to take the law into their own hands, to avenge unpunished crimes. It is interesting that many felt that they would have preferred to carry out the acts of revenge alone, and without assistance. They felt guilty for drawing others into their plans. Thus a sense of social responsibility may be seen as an inhibiting factor in the formation of gangs. Women respondents preferred not to get personally involved and would do so only if no-one else would act. One woman said:

❛ None of my brothers seemed prepared to do anything about this, so I felt that I had to do it myself. I worked with my sister, and we managed to buy a gun, and are practising shooting for the time when they [the perpetrators] return. ❜

By addressing the traumatic experiences which lie at the heart of the distress and anger that characterise these young people, it is possible to influence the process that leads to the formation of gangs in the community. The mere act of talking to a skilled facilitator about the original traumatic experiences has a considerable impact upon their behaviour. In both the cases quoted above, counselling has led to the abandonment of the respondents' plans to seek revenge for past injustices.

A second important finding relates to family pressures and expectations. A critical mediating factor seemed to be the role of family members following a traumatic experience, and even in cases where there had been no prior trauma. All respondents not involved in crime said that they felt accepted by their family and community, and mentioned the fact that their parents served as role models. Those who had been involved in gangs did not mention parents as role models, or family support or community acceptance. Those who had discontinued their involvement in crime named as role models people who were relatively new in their lives, particularly youth-group leaders in the community and facilitators from the KZN-PSV.

In the case of those who had survived traumatic experiences, the way in which the family handled the event, and the person's feelings about the event, seemed critical. People who were not encouraged to talk about their feelings or about what happened felt alienated from their support system. This made them more likely to seek support elsewhere, by becoming involved in gangs. Many spoke of their involvement in crime as a means of expressing their anger against their families.

An interesting and unexpected finding is that the formation of gang-like youth structures is linked to factional violence within the community. One small rural community had two clearly identifiable groups of young men who moved around the community together. There were sporadic outbreaks of violence between the groups, especially in connection with traditional rituals and ceremonies. The youths were grouped into these gangs according to family name and history. On further investigation, it was found that they were feeling pressurised by their parents to operate in this way. Most of the parents had been involved in similar fighting in their youth, and still bore the grudges of the past, expecting their children to carry out revenge attacks and align themselves accordingly. If the young people expressed a willingness to be connected with their peers from the other side, they would be severely berated by their family and face ostracism. One young woman from this community said: '*I am tired of carrying on like this. This is the war of our parents. It is not our war, and yet we are being expected to carry it out.*'

Even in cases where there had been no evident prior trauma, young people were influenced by the expectations and pressures imposed on them by their parents. Young men, in particular, felt expected to provide for their families economically. Many received harsh words from their parents about their personal worth. One young man said: '*When I got my matric, my mother quit her job. She said it was now up to me to take over the support of the family. She became very angry when I did not get a job immediately, and I feel guilty and helpless.*'

In consultations with local community leaders, it was noted that leaders often alienate young people by their unrealistically high expectations of them. One leader recently commented: '*I think we add to the anger and hopelessness of the youth. We do not include them or speak to them respectfully.*' Another leader said: '*The youth around here are just useless. They are good for nothing. They just sit about all day and expect jobs to fall in their laps. Then they get involved in gangs, and turn against us.*' Thus although economic issues are an important predictor of youth involvement in violent crime and criminal gangs, it is most influential in combination with high (and often unrealistic) expectations on the part of adults within the family and broader community. It is an unavoidable fact that in KwaZulu-Natal today it is extremely difficult to find work, particularly for those who are poorly educated and lack marketable skills.

The importance of social identity and belonging, a common finding in research on gangs and youth crime, was confirmed in our research. Many respondents report very positively on their involvement in youth groups, sports clubs, church groups, or some other relatively formalised youth structure. This was especially true for young people who felt unaccepted following their involvement in violence and trauma. One youth-group member said:

> ❦ 'Coming here each week gives meaning to my life. I spend much of my week thinking about the group and the last meeting, as well as the next meeting. This keeps me occupied, and less frustrated about my life.' ❧

Another said: '*It is good to feel that I belong somewhere. Before, I felt like an outcast, and I longed for that acceptance.*' In describing the activities of these youth structures, respondents mentioned the value of clear goals, membership fees, and clear guidelines for conduct in the group. The importance of working towards something that benefits not only themselves but also their community was mentioned several times.

Whether criminal gangs meet a similar need for their members is less than clear. Certainly gangs provide some sense of justification for acts of violence relating to anger and revenge, as well as the means to commit such acts. However, the structure of gangs in these communities is less formal than might be expected from international research. Nevertheless, there is clear evidence of the operation of dress codes and some initiation rituals. Often particular (and expensive) brand names were involved. One respondent wrote: *'To join, you had to be known as somebody prepared to assault people ... We wore red All Star tackies, red t-shirts, black jerseys and a black cap. People in the community knew this and were scared of us.'*

Contrary to popular belief, young people did not experience much difficulty in leaving gangs, and no formal register of members is kept, although affiliations are well known. The need to find another source of income seemed an acceptable reason for leaving the group, although some were subject to abuse. It seemed that the main problem was the threat of disclosure of information about criminal activities to the police. Where people are trusted not to endanger the group, there is less danger of repercussions upon leaving.

The gangs also seem to provide a means of support and protection for intended acts of violence. The status of gangs seems to be reinforced socially, as gang members are seen as powerful. One young woman commented: *'I'd far rather go out with someone from a gang. They have money, and when they get it, they spend it freely. There's none of this talk about budgets and retirement policies that the employed men talk about.'* A woman who was gang-raped repeatedly by the same gang said: *'They are so powerful. They can take any women they want. When he saw me, I knew I could hide and avoid him as long as possible, but he would get me eventually.'*

A young man who had previously been in a gang was asked about the advantages of membership and replied: *'You get status, cars, girlfriends, a nice house, dress in fashionable clothes, and people are scared of you.'* But in a seeming contradiction, it appears that many young men become involved in gangs and violent gang-related activities through a sense of inferiority. One ex-gang member said: *'I used to see these educated black girls, and think to myself "You think you are so superior, but I will show you."'* It would be interesting, although very difficult, to assess the self-esteem of youths involved in gangs. Their level of formal education would also be an important factor. Many respondents cited one of the disadvantages of being involved in a gang as facing alienation from the community, developing a bad reputation, and facing isolation. All cited death, being in danger and constant fear, and going to jail as disadvantages.

An important consideration is that many respondents involved in gangs did not join initially by personal choice. One respondent described being dragged out of his house at night and being forced to kill his friend. This was his enforced initiation, and he had to join the group in order to avoid being killed himself. Most respondents said that they had initially been pressurised to join the gang.

Hopelessness emerged from the study as a key characteristic of many township youths involved in crime. The pressures from family members to provide material support, and their own seemingly failed dreams, have led many young adults to consider joining a gang as a viable strategy to improving their circumstances. Many interviewed in the focus groups and as individuals demonstrated a type of 'tunnel vision' often associated with hopelessness. Several were noted to be missing out on opportunities available to them, and many presented 'yes but' type answers when these opportunities were pointed out. However, through reflection upon their own feelings of hopelessness, young people are able to consider a wider range of possibilities for their futures. The data clearly showed that all people not involved in crime saw a positive future for themselves.

Linked to this, an obvious contributing factor in the problem of gangs and crime is the high rate of unemployment. This was the stated reason for the involvement of several young people in crime. Many young people, particularly those who had successfully completed secondary school, expected to secure immediate employment. Younger children have noted the unemployment of their older siblings, and say that it is useless to get an education, because you will in any case not get a job. Further research into these younger people's attitudes and beliefs would be useful. For many youths it seems that involvement in crime and gangs is a means of securing income for their families, and many consider it their only option.

It was noted that participation in school or further study was an important source of resilience. Many of the young people reported a change in their attitude and beliefs about themselves when they felt that they were engaged in meaningful advancement of their education.

This section has presented an overview of the understanding that the KZN-PSV has developed of young people involved in criminal gangs in the communities of KwaZulu-Natal. Although many of the results were predictable, given the international research, there are also some surprising findings, a fact which illustrates and underlines the importance of first-hand knowledge of target communities. Although the process of becoming intimate with the subtle workings of communities can be extremely frustrating when the need for intervention is so pressing, it is nevertheless indispensable.

There is a danger in South Africa of dismissing factional fighting as unimportant, not unlike the way in which 'black-on-black' violence was dismissed in the 1980s. This would be a mistake, since – no matter what its causes – this kind of violence does enormous damage to the social and economic fabric of rural communities and is directly counter-productive to the work of development.

Developing intervention strategies for gangs

Many community members speak with helplessness about the involvement of young adults in crime, and the rise in gang-related activities in their areas. They seem overwhelmed by the problem, and do not know where to start to tackle it. Yet systematic analysis and further consideration of the clear and consistent themes which have emerged offer a sense of hope for interventions designed to combat the problem. The fact that many of the so-called gangs are not highly formalised structures, and have high rates of turnover, is positive. Many of the young men to whom we spoke did not seem to have such a difficult time leaving the groups to explore alternatives. Others did face severe criticism and described acts of jealousy directed at them. Below are listed the strategies currently being utilised by the KZN-PSV programme to combat these problems. These strategies emerge naturally from the research findings and from the suggestions of the young people themselves, as well as the staff of the programme. As always, in accordance with the action-research policies of the organisation, these strategies are subjected to continuous scrutiny and evaluation, and are modified and developed as appropriate.

Counselling to deal with anger and the urge to take revenge

Since so many of the youth of KwaZulu-Natal have been exposed to multiple traumatic exposure, there is an urgent need for trauma counselling. Most of the young people whom the programme aims to reach harbour feelings of extreme anger, and many feel that the perpetrators of the violence towards them have not been punished. Revenge plans are common, and many are working actively to implement them. The simple process of listening to the stories, hearing the anger and justifiable rage, containing it, and eventually exploring non-violent options is a powerful means of curtailing the involvement of youth in crime and gangs.

Building social-support structures

All adolescents have a need to belong to a group of peers. It seems that where young people do not find acceptance in a group such as a church group, youth committee, or sports group, their chances of becoming involved in a gang-like structure are higher. This was noted especially for those who are not involved in school, further education, or employment. The formation of youth groups that provide mutual support and acceptance is important, and a degree of formalisation seems to be important too: it is useful for groups to think up their own name, develop their own constitution and norms of conduct, print a t-shirt to publicly display their membership, and so on. This group development should be encouraged by non-government organisations, government, and local leadership alike.

Working with parents and community leaders

A large part of previous interventions by the organisation and other service providers has focused on direct work with unemployed, out-of-school youth. While this is important, the research results clearly indicate the need to work simultaneously with their parents and leaders. Sensitising these influential people, and dealing with their own frustrations and failed expectations, is an important way of helping young people to avoid involvement in crime. This may be done through workshops, home visits, consultations, and raising awareness through the media.

Career development

A pilot project involving career development is currently showing promise. Most employment-skills training schemes offer a narrow range of courses, into which young people slot themselves as best they can. Often, not enough

Figure 10 Members of the Siyajabula youth group at Mbovu, Umbumbulu, near Durban, singing in a style called *isicathamiya*.

attention is paid to the trainee's particular aptitudes and interests, or to the job market once the trainee has completed the training. Working on career development helps young people to look critically at themselves, their interests, and their strengths and weaknesses. They are assisted to choose the kind of work they might like to do and explore the feasibility of earning income from that work. Once a feasible goal has been decided upon, plans of getting there can be drawn up. This process provides young people with stronger motivation for developing themselves, and realistic expectations of the challenges that they must overcome.

Testimonies of other young people who have faced similar pressures and hardships are used to inspire participants to explore alternative means of generating income and furthering their aspirations. We have noted that actively exploring various options for further education has positive impacts in terms of increasing young people's sense of direction and self-esteem. For many, such a forceful campaign, especially using the testimonies of peers, seemed to help them to break out of the tunnel vision of hopelessness.

Income generation for young people

Many young people, regardless of their emotional state and level of motivation, have no access to appropriate skills training and continued education. For these people, small-scale income-generating projects become a way of maintaining hope, direction, and self-esteem. Although young people initially join these projects enthusiastically, hoping for quick-fix solutions, many drop out and become disillusioned just as quickly. Long-term commitment to the projects must be carefully fostered. If projects are located within existing youth structures, individuals continue to reap the benefits of belonging to the group during the early stages of the income-generating work. This helps to sustain energy and commitment to the enterprises. Specialisation within the group is also important, to avoid members competing for the same profits.

Collaboration with other agencies

Work with the gangs of KwaZulu-Natal is complex and requires long-term commitment and a degree of technical expertise. It also requires the combined efforts of a range of organisations and concerned structures. With the ambition of working simultaneously at the levels of the individual, the small group, the local community, and society in general, it is essential to develop supportive networks of agencies and advocates. The participation and commitment of people working locally, provincially, and nationally, both within government and in the non-government world, is critical. Despite the inevitable set-backs, the investment of time, thought, and hard work can pay off. In the words of a former gang member:

> ❛ We came to this workshop to escape the arrests happening at the present, because we had been involved in crime. But now we are changed people, and have decided to turn away from criminal activities. We believe this was meant to happen. ❜

Working with youth leaders in civil conflict

In KwaZulu-Natal, as in all other situations of civil conflict, it is young people (mostly men) who are the actual combatants. Typically these teenagers and young adults are organised under similarly youthful leadership, who in turn receive their orders from adult leadership in their community. The KZN-PSV found it impossible to work with the foot-soldiers of these 'teenage armies' without the support of the youth leadership in the community. Youth leaders are typically young men who have been singled out by local political leaders to organise, train, and command young soldiers in the area. And so, when the situation in the province was at its most tense, special intervention strategies were developed for work with these paramilitary commanders.

The youth-leadership programme of the KZN-PSV was centred on the concept of leadership, as opposed to youth development, peace making, or mental health. In this way, the programme was designed to respond to the primary concern of these young people, namely, how to be a good leader. The work with youth leaders included the following components.

- *The challenges facing youth leadership:* This section was designed to allow youth leaders to express the difficulties that they faced in their lives, such as their need to meet the multiple and often contradictory expectations of local political leaders, the youth in their area, their parents and other family members, and girlfriends. In many cases these young men had experienced extremely traumatic events which strongly influenced their capacity as leaders. Learning that they were not alone in these experiences, and that they could continue to function as leaders after talking about them to other leaders, was often important.

- *Analysis of community dynamics:* In this section young people were encouraged and assisted to understand the network of power structures, alliances, and enmities that existed within their own communities. They were encouraged to think about people's stated and hidden motives, and to think carefully about the consequences of various types of action within the community.

- *Developing a personal vision for the community:* Given that youth leaders would be the community leaders of the future, the staff of the KZN-PSV encouraged each leader to develop a personal vision for their own community in the future. As expected, this vision usually involved being at peace, having facilities and infrastructure within the community, and having access to employment.

- *Planning to move towards the vision:* Finally, youth leaders were assisted in drawing up realistic plans to start moving their community towards their personal vision for the community. Consistently these plans contained a core of work towards peace making, community and personal healing, and development – activities which are at the heart of the KZN-PSV's work.

Thus the work of the youth-leadership programme aimed (1) to help young leaders to think more critically about their beliefs and actions, thereby reducing their pliability in the hands of the warring local leaderships, and (2) to win their trust and support, to enable work to be done with other young people in the community. Unsurprisingly this line of work was potentially dangerous. Local political leaders were often highly suspicious of what we were trying to achieve with the youth leaders, and it was necessary to work with extreme care at all times. Nevertheless, it was the work with youth leadership that entrenched the KZN-PSV within warring communities at the most frightening time in the province's recent history.

Conclusion

As the level of conflict has declined and the rigid organisation of young people into paramilitary units has disintegrated, it has become possible for the KZN-PSV to work directly with young people in the community, as was described earlier in the chapter. However, for communities where the level of threat is still high, a less direct avenue of attack is more suitable.

In conclusion, through individual work, work in groups, and participation in youth projects, the community workers of the KZN-PSV are striving to help young people to develop their skills and confidence in order to realise their goals, including restoring peace to their communities. This is done through helping them to master the challenges of adolescence and young adulthood (*empowerment*) and to form productive relationships with their peers, with their families, and with people and organisations in their own community and the broader society (*linking*).

The following is an extract from a poem by a young woman, Philisiwe Gomba, who is starting to reclaim her dignity and vision.

Who the hell are you to call us the lost generation?
Where were you when we needed guidance?
Where were you when we needed you to nourish our delicate minds?
So we say, we were never lost, but ignored.
We were never lost, but deprived.
...
The future is in our hands.
Let us mould what is left of it,
For we can make a difference.
Let us be a rolling stone and gather no moss
For it will cover our beauty.

7 Work with women

'I do not believe that these experiences were meant to break us. They were given to us in order that we might be strengthened. It is the same boiling water that hardens an egg that softens a carrot.'

These words were spoken by a woman from the community of Bhambayi, north of Durban, who participated in a support group for women run by the KZN-PSV for more than three years. Recently she died of AIDS, but she has left these powerful words of resilience and hope. The organisation uses her testimony continually to motivate its own staff and people in all the communities with whom it has contact. Our work with women has been some of the most rewarding and inspiring work that we have embarked upon. The women of Bhambayi have made important strides in taking control of their lives and building their community. For this reason, it is the Bhambayi women's groups that are featured in this chapter.

As with all the work of the KZN-PSV, the women's projects began with a formal request from members of the community. The initial request came from mothers of members of existing youth groups. They had observed positive changes in their children, and asked for similar groups to be established for women in the area. At the time, the community of Bhambayi was entirely divided between supporters of the ANC and the IFP. Through the centre of the community is a wide stretch of abandoned homes, which served as a buffer between the two warring parties. As a result, it was not possible to initiate a Bhambayi women's group that would be accessible to women throughout the community. Although the request for work had come from one side of the community only, in the interests of maintaining our impartial stance it was necessary to establish groups on both sides of the community. These two initial groups began running in parallel, and it was well known to the participants in both groups that the same facilitators were working with women on the other side of the community too. In this way the group facilitators were already starting to break down the rigid lines of division which characterise this community.

The work with women is modelled very closely on the tested model of KZN-PSV's work with youth. Women too were required to take ownership of and responsibility for their own group. They too chose a name, decided upon the content of what they wanted to discuss, and elected group leaders and representatives. The groups met on a weekly basis to work on issues of personal development, community development, and income generation. However, from the earliest meetings it became clear that these women wanted and needed to spend much more time than did the young people in working through their traumatic experiences and grieving for what they had lost. The group process was modified accordingly. As a result, a great deal of time and energy was spent in the women's groups on working through the horror of the civil violence that the members had survived.

The role of women in Zulu society

No single measurement could be used to assess the overall impact of violence on women in this area. Although Zulu society is extremely patriarchal, it is traditionally considered appropriate that women, especially older, married women, are treated with a great deal of respect. The women of Bhambayi felt that this respect had been stripped from them entirely. During the fighting they had been subjected to all kinds of exploitation and been violently used by both political parties. Many recounted tales of emotional abuse and psychological torture which had led them to flee from their homes and communities. A common and recurring theme for these women is a history of being rejected and alienated from friends and relatives. When the community of Bhambayi was torn apart by violence, women lost their place in the broader society and had been unable to find support or friendship among the people of nearby communities. One member of a group expressed her distress in the following words.

> ❛ There are experiences in your life that leave you out of shape on the inside of you. They make you feel like a cloth torn in shreds. ❜

Bhambayi, like many other communities in KwaZulu-Natal, is characterised by high levels of political intolerance. Women in the community have witnessed and perpetrated many crimes of violence against people with different political values or beliefs from their own. The message is clear: *When you disagree with me, you become a non-person. As such you cease to exist as a human being, and I am justified in treating you as an object. As such you may be abused, manipulated, mistreated, exiled, or killed.* This was the logic that the adult men and women of Bhambayi applied to each other during the conflict in the area. Of course, it was also the logic applied to women by their husbands and the other men in their community.

In this climate of threat, mistrust, and insecurity, women were forced to adopt the same political beliefs as their husbands or partners. In many situations this led to the distortion or destruction of the family relationships. Political dissent within families was not allowed, and women who could not conform to this unwritten rule were driven from their homes. Under these circumstances it became extremely difficult for women to carry out their traditional duty of transferring socially responsible morals and values to their children and the broader community. Messages about the need for tolerance, sharing, non-violence, and peaceful conflict management are lost when the broader community is tearing itself apart in revenge killings, destroying and stealing each other's property, and controlling political beliefs through violence. The role of mediator within these troubled families fell constantly to the women, who were unable to manage the conflict and typically experienced enormous distress. Consequently there is a high incidence of anxiety disorders, depression, and alcoholism among women in Bhambayi, and only exceptional individuals have managed to survive these destructive social dynamics with their sense of self intact. More common is tremendous emotional suffering, deep hopelessness, helplessness, loneliness, and loss of meaning and direction. The sense of disempowerment is graphically depicted in the following words spoken in one of the women's groups: *'Our greatest trauma is the realisation that we were caged inside those shacks.'*

The groups' strong focus on traumatic stress and loss gave these women some time for themselves, to rebuild their sense of self, unburdened by the expectation that they should be caring for their families or earning money. Unsurprisingly, this time spent in talking about feelings of trauma, fear, and grief created strong bonds among the women of the groups. Some of them wanted to remain silent, because of their deep-rooted cultural beliefs and traditions. This reluctance to participate actively in the group was a source of frustration to group facilitators and other members of the group, and yet its source was clear and understandable. In some cases, support from other members of the group created a sense of security that was sufficient for these women to share their feelings and experiences with others around them. When this happens, the experience of relief and support is often overwhelming, as people who have been unable to share their feelings before give expression to them for the first time. One woman commented: *'I realised that other people in this group felt the same as me, and we could understand each other.'* Another said:

> Not being listened to and not being heard makes me feel like a thing or an object.

Figure 11 Mrs Mthembu, a member of the Zimseleni women's group, Phindela area, Umbumbulu, weaving a grass mat

Paul Weinberg/KZN PSV/Oxfam

The silence of women, especially those living in rural communities, is common all around the world, and not least in South Africa. The testimonies made to the Truth and Reconciliation Commission (TRC) were mostly submitted by men, despite the Commission's best efforts to encourage women to come forward and give their evidence. Thus, with the exception of a few outspoken women, the recent public history of South Africa remains largely the history of men. Those women who have participated in the TRC have mostly been senior political activists; and, while their stories are critically important, the experience of the majority of women from the townships and rural areas remains virtually unheard and unrecorded. The community-based groups provide one way of building women's confidence to the point when their stories will eventually be heard publicly.

Ethnic divisions within communities in KwaZulu-Natal

Apart from the divisions along political lines, Bhambayi is divided in other ways as well. There are several different ethnic groups within the community, most notably Zulu and Pondo people. Furthermore, within the Zulu majority there are several different clans, between whom relationships are not always good. These ethnic divisions are a further obstacle which prevent the women of Bhambayi supporting each other in the most effective ways. As some members of the group worked through their emotional distress and became more confident, power struggles for control of the group began to emerge. Paradoxically it began to look as though the organisation's work to heal and empower these women was going to result in the destruction of the group and possibly even further injure other women in the groups.

In large part these power struggles were related to the existing ethnic divisions within the community. Each person wanted members of her own ethnic group to be on the women's group's committee and to represent the members on the executive committee of the KZN-PSV. (As noted earlier, half of the executive team of the KZN-PSV consists of representatives of the organisation's beneficiary communities.) Unrelenting intolerance for differing viewpoints emerged once again within the group, and facilitators found themselves constantly working in a conflict-management mode during group sessions.

On a weekly basis the group explored these deep-rooted divisions, and the facilitators worked to resolve the conflicts and prevent the threatened collapse of the support group. Fortunately, enough trust had been established, through the discussions of the shared traumatic history of these women, for the group to be able to grapple with extremely threatening and painful issues. Several factors were identified as lying at the heart of the divisions in Bhambayi:

- the need to establish personal safety by ensuring that one's allies were in positions of authority;
- fear of what would happen if people whom one did not trust were placed in positions of authority;
- fear of being rejected by other members of the group;
- fear of being controlled or dominated by other women in the group;
- feeling alienated from the rest of the group;
- and being anxious that one would not receive a fair share of the resources that were available to the community through the KZN-PSV.

Taken one at a time, none of these issues is particularly surprising or difficult to understand. Taken together, they speak to the way in which years of intolerance, civil conflict, fear, and threat change the way in which people relate to each other at the most fundamental levels. Many of these women have survived for as long as they have by being tougher and more suspicious than the people around them. While such behaviour is necessary for survival during a time of civil conflict, it does not help people's attempts to make the most of opportunities for support and healing when the possibility becomes available.

The challenge for the facilitators in this difficult time of the group's history, which lasted nearly a year, was to remain completely neutral and in so doing to help the group members to hold the group together long enough to explore and learn from the deep issues that divided them. Several members left the group during this time, which was disappointing and frustrating for the community workers. However, the year spent struggling with the issues enabled those remaining eventually to rebuild the relationships within the group, and then within their families, and ultimately within the community at large. More and more, the women of Bhambayi have started to regain their rightful position and respect within the community.

Community healing and individual health

These changes are illustrated by the groups' more recent work. They have been concentrating on issues relating to the health of their community. In the absence of concerned and committed men, the women have forged ahead on their own to discuss issues of reconciliation and healing. They believe that only through healing their community can they create the space for individual healing. And so the women began to organise workshops for community healing, with the aim of ending the fighting in Bhambayi and restoring the unifying community structures that had been destroyed.

This approach to healing contradicts more traditional models of mental-health work, which tend to start with individual healing, in the hope that a community of emotionally healthier individuals will be able to heal itself. Of course it is true that these women would not have been in a position to start the process of community healing themselves without the long personal struggle that each had experienced in the group. In the end, the two approaches are not mutually exclusive. While it is true that there is little hope of helping people to recover individually while their community is still at war with itself, it is also true that it takes people who are resilient and able to manage their own feelings extremely well to work to end the cycles of violence that characterise the history of a place such as Bhambayi. Both kinds of intervention are required, simultaneously and sympathetically.

❛ I used to be an outcast, because I drank heavily. I was frustrated because I have to look after my child, who is blind, and had to leave my job in the sugar-cane farming. But now I belong to the group, and I am respected in the community. ❜

Sadly, the challenges facing women such as the one quoted above are far from over. As the women's groups have assumed greater prominence in the community, so they have attracted the attention of local men. Many men were extremely suspicious of the group and were unhappy to see the women meeting on a regular basis. Some men felt that the discussions might encourage their wives and partners to engage in extra-marital affairs, and men have been known to attend the group meetings in order to make sure that no other men were present.

A particular case illustrates the destructive extent of this dynamic. One woman with a history of abuse by her husband told the group how he had suspected her of having sexual intercourse while she was away from home at the group meeting. He had attacked her upon returning home, and before she could enter the house had forcibly undressed her in public, in order to check whether or not she had indeed had sexual intercourse. The group listened to this story with close attention and then spent several hours debating their response. This alone is evidence of the progress that these women had made. Two years earlier, such treatment would have been accepted by the victim and ignored by other women in the community; but now things were to be different. It was eventually decided that this man should be made to understand that when he humiliated his wife in this way, he degraded every woman in the community. The women arranged to arm themselves with sticks and go together to the perpetrator's house and discuss the matter thoroughly with him. Although the facilitators were not comfortable with this decision, we had committed ourselves to the ideal that the groups should be entirely self-managed, so we could not stand in the way of this controversial choice of action. It was carried out as it had been planned, and – somewhat to the women's surprise – other men in the community did not come to the aid of the perpetrator. In such ways, the women of Bhambayi are actively reclaiming their pride and sense of self. One woman commented: *'These meetings have empowered me so much that I can live independently of a man, and they have helped me to take decisions previously it would have been difficult for me to take.'*

Husbands and boyfriends present many other challenges to the women's groups in Bhambayi. At the height of the fighting, virtually every woman in the community allied herself closely with a man, to ensure some degree of safety for herself and her children, and to secure some means of financial support. As a result, many women have had relationships with the husbands and boyfriends of other women in the group. This has severely affected the dynamics within the group. Such disruption in traditional family relationships has also made step-parenting almost the norm in the community. Many of the younger women in the community were themselves raised by a step-parent. Many cases of childhood abuse and neglect stem from the fact that their biological fathers were absent, and their mothers lived with men who did not care for the children. In response, an important part of the group work has been an exploration of the difference between love and abuse, and how to deal with the conflicting emotions of being dependent upon a man for protection and sustenance, and thereby being vulnerable to abuse by him.

These are all difficult issues, which cannot be neatly worked through in a series of workshops. Nevertheless, the women are becoming more and more assertive and in many cases are starting to share their views within their families and at community meetings without fear. Most men have appreciated the shift in these women, and the resultant change in the way that the community at large is responding to them. More women from the group have been elected to serve in community structures, which has boosted their confidence still further, and reinforced their support for the group.

Paul Weinberg/KZN PSV/Oxfam

Figure 12 Mrs Mbanjwa belongs to the Cabangokuhle women's group, Sweetwaters, near Pietermaritzburg, which has established a sewing project to earn income for its members.

But as women have become more powerful, some men have felt threatened. Some women who were formerly dependent upon the men in their families are now realistically employable and able to earn their own money. In some cases, wives and girlfriends have been prevented from attending the group. The facilitators have been clearly informed by men on more than one occasion that empowering women is 'a waste of energy and resources'.

Other men in the community have responded differently. Recently a group of men have asked KZN-PSV to run a group for them too. For these men to acknowledge the depth of their own distress and their need for support is an important step forwards. In our work with men, we create a space where they can talk about their experiences and feelings and so work towards healing for both themselves and their families. In this way we try to build collaborative and constructive relationships within the community. Most of the men who are today members of this new group are connected either directly or indirectly to one of the women in the women's groups.

Work with children

8

'There is no evil in children. It comes naturally by seeing and doing evil.'

These words, spoken by a traditional healer, illustrate the African belief that children are born pure, but vulnerable. The plight of children in the townships and rural areas of KwaZulu-Natal is an increasingly worrying one. In the generally adverse conditions created by poverty, malnutrition, and poor educational facilities, children with special needs receive little attention. Among this group are those who have witnessed or suffered political violence, criminal violence, sexual abuse, or domestic violence. The challenge for the non-government and government sectors is to provide specialised care in an appropriate form for children at particular risk, whose needs, as reported by a KZN-PSV staff member, are all too evident:

> ❛ When we first started working in Bhambayi, we noticed the children. Babies were left outside in the street during the day, with a bottle and some food nearby. Older siblings were expected to feed them. ❜

The problems seem overwhelming and insurmountable. An extremely high number of children are left unattended during the day, and the frequent and widespread incidence of child sexual abuse, child prostitution, malnutrition, and exposure to scenes of violence and death is a cause for great concern. Many children are living in unhealthily overcrowded conditions, and large numbers are not attending school. Given the extent of these problems, it has been difficult for KZN-PSV to decide where to focus its energies, in a context where the destruction of society itself has made the needs of children a low priority for many sectors of the community. The comments of a seven-year-old and a nine-year-old, both attending PSV children's groups, testify with unconscious eloquence to these needs:

> ❛ My mother never greets me and asks me how I am feeling. But you ask me how I feel. ❜

❝ I cannot come to the group today, because I have a lot of washing that
I have to get done. ❞

The degree of social fragmentation in the communities of KwaZulu-Natal
has shown us that isolated projects focusing on a particular group of children
do not achieve success unless embedded within a community-oriented
approach. Thus the PSV has chosen to work with the community holistically
to improve the conditions of all children, rather than focus attention on
particular needy children within the community. This is an extremely
distressing choice for community workers to have to make. Working to bring
about change to a community is a gradual process which takes many years –
years that children in immediate distress cannot afford. Deciding to expend
scarce resources on long-term objectives in the face of pressing short-term
need is a painful choice. It is essential that community workers should
understand and feel deeply committed to the long-term objectives of the
organisation, to avoid becoming overwhelmed by the immediate need with
which they are constantly confronted.

Developing intervention strategies

In developing intervention strategies for children, several groups with special
needs must be considered. They include homeless children and orphans,
victims of sexual abuse and child prostitution, children living in families with
high levels of domestic violence, and children who have been exposed to
excessive levels of political and criminal violence.

Orphans and homeless children

As a consequence of the extensive political violence in the target areas, many
families have been disrupted, some children's parents have been killed, and
other children have been separated by circumstance from their parents for
many years. As a result, there are many children living on the streets in the
townships. While parents are working or trying to find work during the day,
many children are left unattended. Often very young babies are left in the care
of slightly older siblings. Many parents cannot afford to pay school fees, which
results in the children being unfairly victimised at school. These children stay
away from school and are also to be found on the streets. Finally, the growing
number of orphans whose parents have died of AIDS presents an alarming
problem in KwaZulu-Natal, a province in which 32.5 per cent of women
attending ante-natal clinics in 1998 tested positive for HIV.

Victims of sexual abuse, and child sex workers

Community members in several areas have complained of the prevalence of child prostitution. Orphans may be given accommodation by groups of young men and older single men, to be treated as slaves or sex workers. The high numbers of unemployed people, combined with the lack of adequate child care, also mean that many children are at risk of sexual abuse. Teachers in local schools report increasing rates of children complaining of sexual abuse, even at the hands of fellow teachers. Children who have been abused tend to receive little specialised care. In many cases, if abuse is reported, the perpetrator is expected to pay a penalty fine, and the matter is presumed to be resolved. Very often there is no public apology, and the perpetrator's family may even do the negotiations on his behalf. People have reported a lack of co-operation by police and judicial systems, and many are deterred from reporting crimes by threats from the perpetrators.

Domestic violence

Domestic violence is commonplace in the communities of KwaZulu-Natal. Many men argue that beating spouses and children is culturally appropriate, an attitude that is hotly debated in the province at the moment. Men involved with the KZN-PSV describe their own frustrations and struggles to come to terms with traumatic experiences in their own past history, and report that they are aware of acting out these problems aggressively towards their families. Once again, little is done for children from violent families.

Exposure to political and criminal violence

The organisation's early research in this area was discussed in Chapter 4. The incidence of trauma-related psychological problems among children is undoubtedly extremely high. Many children have witnessed acts of violence, including the killing of members of their families. Many others have been victims of political and gang-related violence, both of which are still extremely prevalent in some areas of the province. Every week, cases involving the exposure of young children to extreme forms of violence are reported to our organisation. Many children are encouraged to keep quiet about what has happened, for fear of the consequences of breaking the silence, and through well-intentioned efforts to help the children to 'recover'.

Services to all these children in need are extremely limited in rural and peri-urban KwaZulu-Natal. The reasons for this are several, and the KZN-PSV had to give careful consideration to the following obstacles to effective intervention when developing a response to this sector of the community.

Numbers of children in need

Poorly planned interventions have in the past been overwhelmed by the sheer number of children in need of specialised care. It is not possible for every child to be referred to an 'expert' in the field, so inevitably local resources must be used. Developing the capacity of local child-care practitioners is often a way of encouraging local case management, with children at particular risk being referred for professional care outside the community.

Lack of effective State interventions

A large part of the problem is the lack of effective State assistance to children at risk. It is extremely difficult for social workers to remove children from an abusive home when the only alternative accommodation for that child is a prison or a 'place of safety' where the danger of abuse is equally high. Teachers and nurses are placed in an impossible position when they become aware that a child is being repeatedly abused and they are unable to get the police, the criminal justice system, or the Department of Social Welfare to respond in an effective manner. Members of these departments themselves complain of having little knowledge of the needs of children, and they have requested more training to help them to deal with the problem.

Any successful intervention in this area must consider developing a more effective network between the community and the various State services. Building the capacity of the appropriate service providers and developing positive relationships between those agencies is a difficult process. And yet a network of committed and effective helpers is essential for the long-term protection of vulnerable children in this province.

In the absence of adequate national and provincial support structures, it is necessary to start developing local structures and initiatives to protect children. Communities are obliged to make their own arrangements, some of which may be extremely innovative and effective. Such projects need the full support of community leadership.

Involvement of local leaders in child abuse

Large-scale awareness-raising events have often been sabotaged by community leaders, as have attempts to deal with individual cases reported to the organisation. We have become increasingly aware of the need to bear in mind that several key leadership figures have been directly implicated in the abuse of children. This includes school principals and teachers, and religious and political leaders. These leaders wield considerable power in their communities, and have the authority to ensure the silence of victims and their families. Any initiative to meet the special needs of children at risk must involve effective collaboration with leadership. Awareness programmes, run in a non-threatening manner, are gradually changing the way in which community leaders treat the problems of child abuse in their areas.

Using community resources

The concept of individual counselling with a stranger from outside the community is alien to Zulu culture. For this reason, clinic-type centres receive very few referrals of children with special needs. Instead, problems are dealt with within families, sometimes with the help of traditional or religious leaders. In many cases, such intervention is highly effective and must be supported and enhanced. Where appropriate, raising awareness about the value of individual or group counselling and case-management practices may be useful, when incorporated into the existing systems and structures.

In its attempt to assist the children of the communities of KwaZulu-Natal, KZN-PSV has engaged in a range of different kinds of work simultaneously. Figure 13 illustrates the way in which work with children is conceptualised.

The adults who support and protect children within communities are the backbone of KZN-PSV's work with children. If these adults can be supported and developed to be able to care for and protect children even more than they are currently managing, a longer-term solution to the challenges of child care

Child Support Services

Child Advocacy	Local Projects	Caregivers	Counselling
— Awareness raising	— Sensitising community to effects of violence on children and caregivers	— Parents	— Individual counselling
— National policy		— Counselling and skills development	— Group trauma counselling and debriefing
	— Rebuilding and supporting existing structures	— Women's groups including economic empowerment	
	— Establishing new structures where appropriate	— Teenage parenting	
	— Networking	— Teachers, crèche workers and volunteer counsellors	
		— Counselling	
		— Skills development	
		— Support and supervision	

SOCIETY   **COMMUNITY**   **SMALL GROUP**   **INDIVIDUAL**

Figure 13: The KZN-PSV model of work with children in violent communities

in the community will have been reached. For this reason, we focus on work with parents and teachers for the remainder of this chapter.

Work with parents

One of the simple hypotheses underpinning our work with children is that addressing the emotional needs of parents in communities affected by violence will have a positive impact on parents' capacity to support and care for their children more effectively. Of course, caregivers are very often not the child's biological parents. Often children are cared for by members of the extended family, especially aunts and grandmothers, or by an older sibling. In virtually all cases, these caregivers are women, so our work with women, described in the previous chapter, has developed in part into work to improve the living conditions of children in the target communities.

There is an immediate dilemma here for community workers. If we continue to support the belief that the care of children is the sole responsibility of women, are we not in turn contributing to the continued drudgery of women in the community? Our struggles with this question have led us to conclude that, since we aim to respond to the concerns and expressed needs of the target community, if a group of women voice concern about the living conditions of children in the community and wish to improve this situation, it would be counter-productive for our community workers to refuse. The needs of children are important, and women in the community are best placed and most skilled to meet some of those needs. But our work with women must never be limited to efforts to create safe conditions for children. Thus the women's projects also tackle a range of other issues – from domestic violence to income generation to community leadership. Finally, there are signs that the women's groups are starting to inspire men to contribute more creatively to their community.

Thus our work with women has become an important aspect of the work to improve the living conditions of children. One particular incident illustrates the effectiveness of this approach. Women told one of the KZN-PSV child-support workers of their concern about a certain young man in the community who was beating his child. A home visit was arranged by the worker, who upon arrival at the house enquired about the man's well-being. He tearfully informed the community worker that his daughter had been sexually abused by another person in the community. He spoke of his rage against the perpetrator and feelings of guilt and self-blame for his failure to protect his child. Having expressed these powerful feelings, he was able to speak calmly with the community worker about his treatment of the child. He explained that she had been acting in a promiscuous manner, which he found difficult to tolerate, because he feared that she would again be abused. He had realised that people had seen him beating the child, and this was adding to his personal shame. With this said, the community worker was able to explain that children respond in individual ways to being sexually abused, and explored with him alternative ways of changing his daughter's behaviour.

Training in parenting skills was also attempted, but the traditional training approaches had to be radically modified, since the parents seemed unreceptive to the usual didactic input on child-rearing practices. Instead, caregivers were encouraged to talk about their own parenting experiences, and what they had found painful, difficult, or useful. Only when sufficient space had been provided for the expression of the parents' own feelings were links made to current parenting practices. One woman spontaneously remarked:

> ❛ I have just realised that the things I hated about my parents' treatment of me are the same things I am doing to my children. ❜

The realisation that one has made errors as a parent is extremely hurtful and distressing. KZN-PSV works hard to help parents to see that finding the courage to try to be a better parent, despite one's own history and the challenges of contemporary society, is heroic. By building confidence and self-esteem, it is possible gradually to modify one's parenting behaviour. The use of traditional and cultural parenting practices is also discussed.

Paul Weinberg/KZN PSV/Oxfam

Figure 14 Members of the Sibonelosihle young single parents' group taking part in a workshop, Phindela area, Umbumbulu

One way in which parents can work to create better living conditions for children within the community is through co-operation in the work of child care. In Bhambayi, women were concerned about the high numbers of children left unattended during the day. In response to this problem, the women decided to establish their own child-care facility. The women involved in this project were given specialist training in child care and early childhood development by the KZN-PSV and other non-government organisations working with children.

Sadly, the broader disempowerment and fragmentation within the community has constantly disrupted the effectiveness of this work. Continuing tensions between and within political parties have been evident in these projects, and outbreaks of violence have repeatedly led to the discontinuation of the services. These problems have been compounded as women running the projects have been increasingly able to take advantage of skills training and externally provided resources, so that managing the facilities has become an important source of income for them. The increased capacity and income of these women incites envy among other people in the community. This has at times resulted in women who are starting to take control of their lives becoming alienated from their families and other women in the community. When people with power within the community become envious, the work that these women are doing can be destroyed.

When the child-care facilities are functioning, children in the community are provided with a safe place to play and learn, they participate in structured and regulated activities, and they receive at least one proper meal each day. In addition, their caregivers are able to attend to other responsibilities, including income generation, which may take them out of the community. However, when the projects are unable to function because of other dynamics within the power structures of the community, this protective environment is taken away from children, and they are forced, temporarily at least, to fend for themselves on the streets. These problems underline the necessity of working simultaneously with multiple sectors within the community. In communities with a history of civil conflict, the process of reconstruction is a long and frustrating struggle.

Work in schools

A second crucial group of adults involved with children are school teachers and principals. Our efforts to develop more integrated and systemic interventions with children in communities affected by violence led to increased work with caregivers in schools. The situation of the schools in these communities tends to be difficult, with multiple problems requiring attention during intervention. These include the teachers' poor motivation, sexual abuse of children by teachers and even principals, abuse of children and teachers by youth gangs, acts of politically motivated violence being perpetrated in schools, and an extreme lack of resources for huge numbers of children.

As in its other initiatives, the KZN-PSV strives to work as holistically as possible in its projects with schools. The aim of the programme in schools is to facilitate development of the entire school community, including learners, teachers, administrators, and parents.

Approaching the schools regarding possible intervention seems to be one of the most sensitive and crucial parts of the intervention. Staff recall a recent visit to one school in an area very sharply divided by violence. It was clear that teachers from both sides of the conflict taught at the school, and this divide was institutionalised at the school. The teachers hardly greeted the KZN-PSV staff, and made no secret of their hostility and suspicions about the proposed project. The community workers spent much time engaging the teachers in social conversation, and eventually tried to introduce the organisation's objectives in a sensitive manner. They listened carefully to the teachers' fears and encouraged them to express their concerns openly. Once again, attempts to understand people's experience at a deep level are at the core of the success of the KZN-PSV.

A needs-assessment exercise is carried out in each school, and a particular intervention is then designed for that school with the governing body. Very often this intervention involves training work with teachers, governing bodies, and learners. Training work with teachers in particular can be extremely sensitive, owing to their particular psychological problems and social positions.

The psychological position of teachers

Most teachers working with the KZN-PSV have themselves been exposed to numerous traumatic events, either directly or indirectly, and have been negatively affected by traumatic stress. Those who have tried to be supportive to children in their care are often suffering from secondary traumatic stress themselves, as a result of the seemingly endless list of horror stories which they have heard. The schools have played an important role in many conflict situations, and children in schools report a range of violent incidents (including sexual and domestic violence) to teachers.

Caring for survivors of violence involves being open to the traumatic experiences of others, but many teachers lack the emotional resilience to offer this service to children in their charge. Very often teachers are severely disempowered by their own traumatic histories and are thus prevented from fulfilling their role as educators and role models to children. So before teachers can begin to serve as caregivers for children, they need assistance in coming to terms with their own experiences, particularly where these affect their capacity to teach effectively. Thus the work with teachers offers them opportunities to reassess their own emotional responses to teaching, and to the schools and the pupils, and to process their own experiences in a secure and supportive environment.

The social position of teachers

The social position of teachers is an extremely difficult one in many cases. Far from being highly respected members of the community (as was the case historically), many teachers are now viewed as outsiders who are not to be trusted. This has come about since teachers were assigned to teaching posts in conflict-ridden communities, where any stranger, including a teacher from the city, is perceived as a potential threat. As a result, teachers typically receive very little support from parents and other community structures.

Moreover, with the high numbers of young people involved in civil conflict, the teachers find it extremely difficult to maintain control and exert authority within the school. Where young people are trained to use weapons and have experienced civil war, the usual methods of classroom discipline lose their effectiveness. In many cases, discipline has been taken over by student representative committees and in some cases even by the political leadership. Often punishment administered in this way would be far heavier than anything ordinarily occurring within schools. In this regard, teachers are unable to fulfil their role as either authority figures or protectors of children.

The fact that teachers are not respected, either by parents or by pupils, makes it extremely difficult for them to offer any kind of emotional support within the schools. For teachers to become more effective in their work, it is important that they are empowered to forge useful links with parents and to recapture pupils' respect. This can be achieved only through a range of simultaneous processes:

- facilitating communication and co-operation between teachers, parents, and other education structures locally;
- helping teachers to explore effective ways of maintaining discipline and gaining respect within the classroom;
- working with head-teachers and the education system to support and assist teachers in these matters.

The development of the schools programme has been an on-going process for KZN-PSV. One of the critical debates has been whether or not to focus on one school at a time, dealing with the whole staff, learners, and parents, or whether to encourage linking with other schools, by selecting a few teachers from each school for joint training. The organisation is moving increasingly to working with one school community at a time. This creates the possibility of offering longer-term support, understanding the challenges facing a school at a deeper level, and creating on-going training and development opportunities. As neighbouring schools observe the positive effects of the organisation's work, they too can participate in the project, and the work of building networks of schools begins.

A second important debate centres on school safety and the relationship between the school and the broader community. There seem to be two major approaches to school-safety programmes: the inclusive and the exclusive. The exclusive approach emphasises practical security measures, such as security fences and weapons checks at the entrances to schools; it is designed to secure the school and prevent negative influences from the external community finding their way inside. An inclusive approach concentrates on establishing open and trusting relationships between the school and the surrounding population, thereby making the safety of the school an issue for the whole community, rather than merely for the school. The latter approach fits more comfortably with the overall vision of the KZN-PSV and is the approach that the organisation has adopted.

The initial stages of the schools project concentrate on building positive relationships with the various stakeholders in the school, including the principal, the teachers, and representatives of students', parents', and staff structures. After initial meetings with the head and governing body, an awareness work-shop and needs-assessment exercise with the whole staff are arranged. Then the staff are encouraged to assist in developing a strategy for helping the school to move towards its goals. A core component of the project is the training of staff; the group decides what training is required, who should be involved initially, and who should be trained at a later stage. Most schools select a group of teachers for initial training, which is then followed up by similar work with members of the school governing body (usually parents and community leaders), and eventually learners.

The content of workshops varies somewhat between schools, but it includes an analysis of the school and community violence, effects of violence and cycles of violence, identification of children affected by violence, and social support work. The groups are encouraged to develop preventative interventions promoting school safety, and action plans are followed up on a long-term basis. For example, a particular school might wish to focus attention on physical abuse of children in the school. Action plans would include running a short course to help teachers, parents, and other members of the school community to identify the signs of physical abuse. In addition, the school would determine in advance the most appropriate referral agencies for child-abuse cases in their area. Finally, the school would run a programme in all the classes, encouraging children to speak out about abuse in their homes. Each of these components is potentially extremely problematic, and the staff of the KZN-PSV would assist the school community to resolve the problems that they encountered.

Building a network of child care

Although work with caregivers, teachers, and other adults in the community is the most important contribution to the longer-term health of the community's children, the current situation of many children in these communities is too urgent to ignore. For those children whose families have been murdered or whose experiences have left them struggling to regain their path of normal development, the KZN-PSV runs weekly groups in several communities. During these sessions, children are involved in developmentally appropriate games which encourage them to interact with other children of their own age, and allow them to slowly process the traumatic experiences that they have survived. These groups are run by a specially trained child-care worker and supervised by a clinical psychologist.

The goal of all this work is to create an environment which supports the development of young children into healthy adolescents and eventually adults. This requires that communities become safe environments for children to live in, and that children receive the physical, emotional, social, and spiritual care that they need. Ultimately, it is not sufficient that this environment exists only in isolated places like child-care facilities and schools. It is necessary that whole communities become environments that promote healthy development.

A step towards this goal is created by bringing together adults who are concerned about children at a local level. This is achieved through Children's Needs Forums. Trained people within the community are encouraged to establish a forum to consider the needs of the children in their community. The task of this forum is to monitor and identify children at risk, refer them for specialised care, assist local welfare agencies in finding placements for them, and provide on-going support to its members, many of whom are them-selves service providers. The forum may also focus on the additional needs of local schools and child-care facilities. It may become a valuable source of further training, for example in general parenting skills and parenting skills relevant to children affected by violence. Finally, these forums have a powerful role to play in local advocacy and awareness raising. Until the rights of children are placed firmly on the agendas of all local government structures, service providers will continue to struggle to support children who are forced to survive in a hostile and damaging environment.

Figure 15 Nothando (left) and Sbu (right) from Bhambayi, attending a children's workshop

Paul Weinberg/KZN PSV/Oxfam

9 Work with community leaders

The work of KZN-PSV described up to this point has all been done in the townships and villages with ordinary people, struggling to prosper in extremely difficult circumstances. But we would be deluding ourselves if we believed that communities could be rebuilt and violence prevented without addressing the dynamics beyond and between particular communities. One way of moving beyond the local context is to create a leadership forum.

The idea of bringing together local leaders from a range of communities to talk about and (ideally) begin to resolve their problems and concerns is not a new one. Sadly, it has not been particularly successful in KwaZulu-Natal in the past. On 14 September 1991, a National Peace Accord was signed by the ANC and IFP, as well as 27 other bodies, including government and trade unions. The Accord aimed to reduce violence and create the proper climate for negotiations. It included a code of conduct for political organisations, prohibiting coercion and committing the signatories to political tolerance, a code of conduct for the South African Police, and various measures for investigating police misconduct. Local peace committees were set up, to bring leaders together in an attempt to resolve conflicts, and teams of monitors began work throughout the province.

Although the Accord was an important step towards a negotiated peace between the ANC and the IFP, it has taken a long time for those agreements to be implemented within local communities. In fact, before long some peace committees became public platforms for accusations and recriminations, rather than peace making. In numerous cases, peace-committee representatives were implicated in attacks and killings, and in some instances were themselves targeted. In 1994 two representatives from Umbumbulu were murdered. It was clear that the structures were not fulfilling their envisaged function; within a few years the budget of the National Peace Accord was no longer supported, and it ceased to operate.

The idea of a leadership forum

So what is different about the leadership forum facilitated by KZN-PSV?

Firstly, it was established at a different, more stable time. Secondly, it was established to respond to the expressed needs of leaders and was not imposed upon them. Most particularly, the project was initiated by leaders of the target communities in which KZN-PSV already had a great deal of credibility and history: our story had become entwined with that of the community. Thirdly, and very importantly, all parties concerned had a clear idea of what they wanted to gain from the project.

From an assessment of the position of many local leaders in KwaZulu-Natal, it becomes clear why the leaders of Bhambayi and Umbumbulu approached the staff of the KZN-PSV for assistance. At a time when the structures of local government are being completely rebuilt, when old political and paramilitary allegiances are very powerful, and when the role of traditional leadership is being contested, governing a community is no simple matter at all. Within both these communities (and the others in which the KZN-PSV is working), a range of governing structures operate. They include democratically elected local councils; traditionally appointed *amakosi* (who have social, political, and economic powers and responsibilities) and *indunas* (responsible for local administration); development committees and forums, consisting of a range of local and external stakeholders; political-party offices; the paramilitary structures attached to political parties; and civic structures. In many cases these various structures compete for popularity, influence, and power within the community, and so relationships between them are often strained and volatile. However, where leaders of these various structures can work together effectively, their diversity and co-ordinated resources can be powerful agents of change. Sadly this has not been the case in these communities, with their long history of war and betrayals. Much more characteristic of the internal power dynamics of KwaZulu-Natal communities are power struggles which sometimes spill over into violence, competition for resources, the marginalisation of important role players, and other equally unconstructive conflicts. Progress in peace making, decision making, and development is consequently very slow; community members become frustrated and disillusioned with their leaders, and leaders feel unsupported or undermined.

Community leaders had seen the work that was being done by KZN-PSV in the youth groups and women's groups; they had observed the progress that people in their communities were making – progress not only in terms of their personal situations, but also in their capacity to organise themselves, collaborate, and manage projects. Youth groups and women's groups were developing a more sophisticated understanding of the functioning of committees, the roles of committee members, ways of running meetings, facilitating groups, and reaching consensus decisions. They were also grappling with

Natal Witness

Figure 16 Members of the Imbali Peace Committee, pictured at Plessislaer Police Station in 1995

questions of good leadership, project planning and implementation, and ways of accessing resources both within and beyond the immediate community. With these new skills and experience, they were gradually starting to get things done and to make a difference to community life.

The sectors of the community that are traditionally least organised and most powerless were starting to run enterprises such as vegetable gardens, income-generating *spaza* shops (small roadside convenience stores), a crèche, and income-generating beadwork projects. In contrast, many development committees throughout KwaZulu-Natal and in other parts of South Africa have been unable to transcend the local tensions that threaten their work, and have made very little progress towards their ideals. Mandated with the task of planning and managing community-development projects, many such committees have been plagued by in-fighting and paralysed by inefficiency and lack of capacity. For these reasons, the leaders of Bhambayi and Umbumbulu sought out the assistance of the KZN-PSV, with a very clear idea of what they hoped to gain from a leadership project.

At the same time, the KZN-PSV had a range of important reasons for wanting to work more closely with local leaders. Up to this time, most of the contact between the organisation and community leaders had been of the official sort: workers met with leaders to seek their permission to work in the community, to inform them of what they hoped to achieve, and to get their public support for their interventions. Leaders are a vital source of information and advice during the planning phases of new projects, but leaders themselves had never been directly involved in our work.

All the people involved with the KZN-PSV were frustrated and worried by the regular outbursts of violence in the target communities, and the fact that the continuing lack of communication between leadership structures was likely to make the problem worse in the near future. This project provided an opportunity to modify the dynamics within and between local structures and, through capacity-building training and facilitated discussion and negotiations, a chance to build constructive local relationships and strengthen the tenuous peace which had been established.

Another reason for wanting a stronger alliance with community leaders was that it would provide field staff with a greater understanding of the challenges facing local leadership, and insight into the difficult relationships between local structures. A stronger link would provide more and better information to guide the range of projects being conducted in that community, which would have positive effects upon the impact and efficiency of these projects. Finally, the initiative provided an opportunity to involve leaders directly in some of the projects within their communities. A local campaign against child abuse is much more effective when prominent leaders are involved and publicise their commitment to the issue.

When described in this manner, it seems strange that it took so long for a project of this nature to get underway. Of course there are reasons for this, and it was truly not feasible at an earlier time. The alliance was eventually made possible by the fact that leaders were beginning to trust the staff of KZN-PSV and to value our work at a deeper level. This trust was earned through reliable and competent work over an extended period of time. The demands on political leaders in a situation of civil conflict are often contradictory. Their success as leaders depends upon their ability simultaneously to protect the community (which involves maintaining a paramilitary force) and to bring an end to existing conflicts (which involves demilitarising the community). Any work that aims to bring peace must require opposing leaders to start talking to each other. Being seen to be talking to the enemy can cost a leader his or her position within the community, unless the situation is handled extremely carefully. It is not surprising that it took time for local politicians to gain confidence in the motives and methods of our organisation.

A second important factor was the way in which the style of local leadership was changing in many of our target communities. Where communities have lived under threat for an extended period of time, it is not surprising that highly authoritarian (and often violent) leaders emerge. Such leaders cannot afford to show weakness and do not collaborate comfortably with others. Furthermore, this style of leadership is not replaced overnight when the threat is diminished. However, with lasting peace becoming an increasing reality in KwaZulu-Natal, more democratic local leaders are gradually emerging. This is in large part due to the challenge of community members themselves, who demand responsible government from their leaders. An important part of KZN-PSV's action has been implicit and consistent support for this demand. The emerging democratic leadership is much more willing to admit to weakness and is keen to collaborate with organisations that have particular resources, in order to achieve the greatest good for their community. These changing dynamics provide new opportunities for work with leaders.

Despite these changes, this project was never going to be simple. Old enmities die hard, especially when constantly reinforced by desperate competition for extremely scarce resources. It was critically important for us to think long and hard about ways of taking this project forward which would not jeopardise the peace and progress that had already been achieved in these communities. We determined to work very cautiously, especially in the light of past failures.

Strategic planning

Most importantly, we needed a plan (and contingency plans) if we were to stand any chance of getting this right. This plan had to answer a range of critical questions, including the following:

- What communities should be involved?
- What structures from those communities ought to be involved?
- How would invited people be approached?
- Where should meetings be held?
- How often should meetings be held?
- What should the format of meetings be?
- How should we deal with participants who disrupt or endanger the process?

The first question was resolved relatively easily. Deciding to start small, we approached only the two communities that had made overtures to us first. These were also convenient, since they were easily accessible to our community workers, and existing relationships with local leaders were good. Next we began to consider the more subtle question of who from those communities ought to be involved. Since there was a range of possibilities in each community and extremely complex histories and dynamics to consider, we decided to think about the problem in terms of the underlying issues, rather than the existing structures. The underlying issues involve competition between differing political party structures in both communities, competition between democratically elected local government and traditionally appointed local government, and between local government and development-committee structures. By keeping the project as open as possible and inviting all interested role players, but insisting on representation from each of the sectors mentioned above, we aimed to protect the process against public allegations of bias. In fact, we tried to invite a specified number of representatives from each of these sectors.

Then, since the lasting success of this project depended largely on leaders taking ownership of the project, we agreed that the organisation's role in the beginning would be to facilitate the development of a shared understanding of the purpose of the project and to help the group to reach consensus on a code of conduct, ways of ensuring that members maintained the code, the content of meetings, the location, frequency, and management of meetings.

With this plan in place, a letter was drafted, inviting a wide range of representatives to an initial meeting on the neutral but familiar ground of KZN-PSV's office in Durban. The fact that the community leaders wished to use the organisation's space as a meeting ground is an important indicator of the degree of trust that had been built, and the clear position of neutrality that the organisation had managed to build for itself. Care was taken to meet personally with leaders from all the different interest groups (party political, council, development committee, and traditional leadership structures), to ensure that all were represented. Equal numbers of leaders from both sides of the conflict were invited.

The first meeting

The initial letter was designed to understate the importance of this project. It stressed that the meeting was to explore the extent of local interest, and emphasised that the original idea had come from leaders themselves; but it included our wish to build a stronger relationship with the people who governed the communities in which we were working. Finally, it was emphasised that a person's literacy level or ability to speak and understand English would not affect his or her ability to participate in the project. This letter was written in English and Zulu, and delivered by hand where possible.

All leaders responded very positively, saying that such training was badly needed. It is interesting that this was the first time that the word 'training' had been used explicitly, and we were excited by the apparent willingness to learn. In all cases, leaders were asked whether they would object to participating in this project with leaders from other political parties and other communities. All agreed, provided that the venue was a neutral one; our suggestion of using our own office was immediately supported. Reminders were sent out one week prior to the meeting, since we were still very anxious that some sectors would not be represented, and would thus lay the process open to accusations of bias. Negotiations thus far had taken approximately two months.

Finally the day came, and more participants than expected arrived: some groups had disregarded their allocated numbers. It was very difficult under such circumstances to send people away, and so we took the risk that the other representatives would accept this at the first meeting. Immediately there were tensions, and we would have been naive to expect otherwise. Some of these concerned travel arrangements, with some leaders feeling that they ought to have been picked up from their homes, and others refusing to travel in the same vehicle as leaders from different structures. It took two hours longer than we had expected to get everyone seated and quiet in the same room. However, despite these problems the mood was very positive, and all parties began by endorsing the need for this type of intervention. This was a crucial step, since if any party had refused to be part of the process, we would have had to make some very difficult decisions about whether or not to continue. Some leaders expressed their feelings of insecurity about the changing demands of leadership. A woman in the group had the courage to open her heart in the following way:

> ❛ We have been elected into these positions, and we have had no proper training. We make decisions which end up hurting people, because they were bad decisions. We did not mean to hurt people, but it happened because we did not have the proper skills. It is time for us to take on the responsibility of leadership and to acquire these skills, so that we can stop hurting each other and the people we serve. ❜

At this point the group burst into spontaneous applause, and the extremely anxious field staff of the KZN-PSV started to breathe a little easier. Having surmounted this difficult emotional hurdle, it became easier to progress. We began to explore areas of particular concern and interest. A long list was trimmed and arranged in order of importance to the participants. It included general leadership skills and styles, facilitating meetings, the roles and responsibilities of members of a committee or team, making community empowerment a reality, planning and managing projects, fund-raising and accessing resources outside the community, conflict management, and solving the problems of youth crime.

From there the group moved on to think about some regulating norms of behaviour for participants. These norms included the necessity of confidentiality, committed and punctual attendance, respecting others' opinions, and listening attentively. Although we were not sure whether this would be sufficient to sustain the process, it was enough that the group had taken responsibility for monitoring their own behaviour, and we would assist them in dealing with more difficult dynamics at a later stage.

Finally the logistics of group meetings were discussed. It was decided that meetings would take place on a twice-monthly basis on the same day of the week, at the same time, and in the same venue. Since the staff of the KZN-PSV had been assuming a system of monthly meetings, it was necessary to reallocate some organisational resources in order to be adequately prepared.

On-going meetings

The first few meetings were characterised by a very positive mood and a great deal of enthusiasm for the project. This 'honeymoon phase' is typical of the experience of many new groups. It is important, because it creates time for the group to get to know each other and start to develop the deeper trust which is the most vital component for dealing with more threatening issues. It was also a time for the group to get used to the experiential learning techniques employed by KZN-PSV in all interventions. This caused some tension, with one participant saying that he had expected to be taught things by the facilitators. We allowed the participants who had a deeper understanding of our methods and experiential learning to lead a discussion about adult education and the principles of empowerment. Although not convinced at the time, this member referred to the style much later in the process, saying how much he was learning.

Each session was run as a formal meeting, with an opening statement and welcome, apologies for absence, review of previous minutes, negotiation of the agenda, main points of discussion, a time for general discussion, and a formal conclusion with thanks. All learning took place through group discussions (either in plenary sessions or small groups) with small amounts of theoretical input. Handouts were requested but kept to a minimum, out of respect for the less literate participants. Each meeting was conducted in Zulu, but minuted in Zulu and English. Minutes were reviewed at the start of each meeting, to remind participants of the reasons for the project and to establish a continuing process.

Issues arising

The first challenging issue to arise came in a slightly unexpected form. Participants started to question why they could meet and talk together constructively at leadership forum meetings, but on return to their own communities tended to cut themselves off and refuse to negotiate. Although this question relates to a range of concerns, it took the group rapidly towards looking at their own individual circumstances. The group moved much more quickly to issues of personal development than was originally expected.

At this point in the process, the question of past painful experiences was tentatively introduced by the facilitators, and met with an energetic response. Any resistance disappeared when the topic was framed as letting go of 'baggage' which belongs in the past, in order to become a more effective leader. The group has struggled through this difficult territory repeatedly, as trust continues to grow. Participants have spoken of watching family members dying in front of them, being involved in armed conflict, and being betrayed by neighbours and friends, as well as their own sense of responsibility as leaders. One participant said:

> ❮ I have been carrying around so much anger about my past, and I did not even realise how much it has been affecting me. When you first introduced this idea of talking about the pain, I did not want to face it – it was too painful. But now that I have started, I already feel relieved – like I am unloading it, and it feels like I must now go all the way. ❯

Another commented:

> ❮ I feel like I am taking a weight off – a weight I have been carrying around me for too long. My past has affected even my personal relationships with my family members – like the private rapes I commit with my wife when I get so frustrated and angry that I don't know what to do with myself. ❯

Skills development

The work on personal experiences is blended into additional skills training in each session. In this way, the leaders participating in the programme have spent several sessions discussing topics such as how to manage a meeting when people disagree strongly with each other; what to do when people consistently fail to attend meetings; how to plan a project so that it works well; and so on. For each new skill discussed, participants set themselves 'homework tasks' to be undertaken with their families and communities. For example, if the leaders had been working on how to listen to the grievances of community leaders in a way that was supportive and not dismissive, they would agree to hold a meeting in the community during the next two weeks, when community members would be invited to talk about local problems with their leader. The leader would exercise the skills that had been discussed in the leadership forum and report back to the group at the next meeting. Participants would then discuss what they had experienced with their 'homework'. In this way, leaders are helped to monitor their own progress, and they become more empowered through the observation of their own mastery of difficult tasks.

Eventually the group dynamics settled down, and the leadership forum has gone from strength to strength. With this initial success, a new leadership forum has been established with each new year, and new local leaders are beginning to support the work started by their colleagues. Leaders from Umbumbulu, Bhambayi, KwaMashu, Amaoti, and Mandeni still meet twice a month and have registered the KwaZulu Challenging Co-Op, a local development agency which they hope will speed up the rate at which the economies and infrastructures of their community can be rebuilt.

At the moment, the organisation has a list of people waiting to join the leadership forum. These leaders come from the communities of Embo, Engonyameni, and Richmond. We are also hoping to include leaders from Inkandla in a partnership with work supported by Oxfam GB in that community. The organisation is particularly encouraged by the increased number of women who are emerging as leaders within their area, and who wish to develop their leadership skills through collaboration with KZN-PSV.

Finally, and perhaps most exciting of all, is a recent request from community leaders for training in leadership skills.

> ❛ We see the wonderful work that Survivors of Violence is doing, and we realise that the limited staff capacity will never be able to reach everyone that needs this work. That is why we would like to be trained, so that we may facilitate similar workshops in our areas. ❜

The Year 2000 group of leaders are being trained as leadership trainers. Sustainable 'train-the-trainer' programmes are extremely difficult to manage and so, as in everything else, the KZN-PSV is moving very carefully with this project. However, with thoughtful planning and by laying down a strong foundation, there is no reason why community-leadership development should not continue to be offered by specially trained community leaders. One member of the leadership forum endorsed its work in the following words:

> ❜ This training has not only impacted on my work as a leader, but also on my family relationships. Before, I used to get so frustrated by my past that I would beat my wife and children. Now I understand where this anger is coming from, and I am able to deal with it better. They say I am a different person. ❜

Reflections on the work of the KZN-PSV   IO

'Before KZN-PSV came into this area, I did not think peace was possible.
We used to be terrified to go out at night, but now we visit each other freely.
Before, when you saw a person approaching you, you were instantly afraid
in case it was an enemy. Now when I see someone approaching, I am pleased
– because it is sure to be a friend' (A woman in Bhambayi)

This final chapter highlights the fundamental elements that have contributed
to the success of the work of the KZN-PSV. Most important is an approach to
communities characterised by long-term commitment, care, and thoughtfulness,
and a strict adherence to a set of guiding principles.

Approach to communities

Following an episode or a protracted period of civil violence, the distress and
the needs expressed by the affected communities can be overwhelming. It is
hard for community-development organisations to resist the urge to respond
immediately by embarking upon the first opportunity for intervention that
presents itself. However, to respond in this way is not effective, is unlikely to
achieve lasting change, and may even be dangerous. Although the damage
done to the social and economic fabric of communities may occur in a matter
of hours, the process of rebuilding takes years. The decision to begin work in
a community recovering from the effects of civil violence is a decision with
enormous long-term implications and must be taken with great care. There
are several points to bear in mind.

- Does the organisation have the resources to begin work at a reasonable level
  within a community? An occasional visit from an already overburdened
  social worker is unlikely to provide any useful intervention, and may damage
  the credibility of the organisation in the eyes of the community. If staff are
  already working to full capacity, an increase in their workload will result in
  high levels of stress, a poorer quality of work, rapid burn-out, and high levels
  of staff turnover.

- Is the community in question the one most in need of the organisation's resources? When resources are committed to one community, the extent of potential work in other areas is immediately limited.

- Can the organisation commit these resources to the community for a reasonable period of time? Many NGO operate an annual grants system, which makes it extremely difficult to guarantee lasting support to communities on the ground. Organisations which have a strong financial base are most able to make meaningful commitments to communities in need.

- Do community workers understand the complex dynamics of the community well enough to find the points at which strategic intervention will bring about the maximum lasting improvement to community life? Have community workers explored a range of intervention strategies, and is there sufficient support for the organisation's work within the target community to ensure a reasonable chance of long-term success?

Until these questions are answered, the organisation is not ready to begin a new intervention programme in a target community. During the years of the KZN-PSV's existence, many other short-lived initiatives have come and gone. Some were projects inspired by students in local universities; others have been headed by academics from Europe and the United States of America. While all these people have been well intentioned, the short-term nature of their work, together with a superficial understanding of the communities of KwaZulu-Natal, has meant that in the end their efforts have produced little observable change on the ground.

Principles of community intervention

The principles outlined below are not new, although they are often neglected by practitioners. They are drawn from a wide range of material, including community-development literature, literature on group facilitation, and the literature on traumatic stress and psychological support and counselling. Although most are applicable to a broad range of community work, others are included to cover the added complexities of working with communities that have survived (or are surviving) civil conflict.

Credibility

A range of varied individuals and institutions offer assistance to impoverished communities. However, not all are adequately skilled or informed, and their work may be ineffectual and perceived by community members to be a waste of time and energy. Many communities in KwaZulu-Natal have had experiences of such projects and have become suspicious of their worth. Furthermore, where communities have experienced a great deal of violence, community members and leaders become distrustful of all strangers, including those offering services. It is necessary for practitioners to establish themselves as competent and sympathetic, in order that service provision may proceed. Credibility rests upon three closely related attributes: **competence, information**, and **attitudes**.

First, practitioners must demonstrate to the community at large that they are suitably skilled to offer the services being discussed. Field workers who operate competently, confidently, and efficiently win the trust of members of the target communities more easily. Appearing competent is often extremely difficult when one is entering a community for the first time and is unsure of local dynamics. Field workers who appear overwhelmed by a community's situation do not instil confidence or a sense of hope.

Secondly, practitioners need to demonstrate a knowledge of, or at least a willingness to become familiar with, the local situation. Field workers require a detailed understanding of the community's history, as well as knowledge of key local people. The stories of each community are long and complex and are usually very painful to tell and hear. However, the 'story telling' of the community can be a key component in initiating an effective intervention, in the same way that the recounting of events is a key element of trauma-response interventions with individuals. Also, people who have recently experienced high levels of civil violence in their community often feel as though their experiences will not be adequately understood by 'outsiders'. For these reasons, detailed personal and community histories are not easily obtained. A field worker who has obviously taken the time and trouble to find out as much as possible about past events has laid the groundwork for an understanding of such histories and so becomes a much more credible witness to events in the community and thus a more effective community worker and peace maker.

Thirdly, it is necessary to demonstrate compassion for the historical and current problems of the community. It is important that community members, and especially leaders, are reassured that their past actions will not be exposed and criticised through the proposed intervention.

A credible practitioner is one who can demonstrate competence in the necessary skills, detailed knowledge of the community, and sensitivity to the community's history and current position.

Maintaining impartiality

A sympathetic understanding of a community's position brings its own problems, especially where an organisation is working with several communities in conflict with one another. One cannot simultaneously maintain an empathetic understanding of two communities who are at war with each other without understanding the broader societal issues that have resulted in these two communities being in conflict. It is sometimes difficult to remember that the true sources of conflict lie outside local situations, and field workers need opportunities to resolve these complex issues properly. For this reason, KZN-PSV attaches great importance to regular and intensive support and supervision of field staff. The following are the paraphrased words of one senior and experienced member of the project staff, describing her interaction with a community leader.

> ❧ He took me by the hand, and we walked around the community together greeting everybody. He clearly wanted to be seen in my company. But when he touched me, I could not stop thinking of all the terrible things he has done. My skin crawled and I wanted to pull away, but instead I had to walk around the community with him, smiling at all the people. ❧

However, more difficult than simply maintaining impartiality is *demonstrating* impartiality. This can be achieved only by adopting a clear public policy of working on both sides of the conflict – and then doing so. Only by monitoring the number of visits, the number of projects, and the level of resources being devoted to particular communities can absolute impartiality be maintained. Regular meetings with community leaders and other local structures can be used to make it very clear that work is being undertaken equally with all parties. Experience, however, has frequently shown that one of the warring communities is easier to work with than the other. This can swiftly develop into a situation where more work is done with one party than with the other. When this happens, impartiality is sacrificed. Even when one community seems less well resourced than another, equal distributions of resources (especially staff time) may need to be made. Maintaining impartiality is a difficult process, needing continual attention.

Never suggesting that people are ill

Working within a psychological framework brings with it the danger of thinking about survivors of civil violence as being ill, or deficient in some other sense. If we make the assumption (often automatic and implicit) that people who have experienced extreme levels of violence must be in need of support and assistance, we can fall into the ubiquitous trap of pathologising them. The provision of support and assistance to victims of civil violence must be a response to expressed distress on their part, or prompted by a shared desire to resolve some practical problem facing the community. Development workers must always be alert to the possibility that their motives will be misinterpreted by survivors of civil violence. The events of an early youth-leadership training programme illustrate this. During a session, one young man discovered a facilitator working from a manual which had the word 'transformation' in the title. In fact it referred to the transformation of society and the removal of structural inequalities, but the young man understood the title to suggest transforming people's personalities and values. He managed to get himself and the other participants extremely distressed and angry, very nearly destroying the entire project on the basis of his misinterpretation and sensitivity. This was an important lesson to everyone involved in KZN-PSV: that we can never be too careful not to pathologise the people and communities with whom we work.

Showing respect

Respect is an attitude which grows as the story of an individual, family, or community is heard. For this reason, attentive and open-minded listening is one of the most important characteristics of the successful community worker. It is likely that the choices and concerns of people who have been exposed to and survived intense civil conflict will not coincide with the expectations of community workers. For example, when a mother is forced to choose between sending a child to school and feeding him or her, a community worker who assumes that the child is being inadequately parented is not demonstrating an attitude of respect. More careful listening usually yields a story which explains the situation and places mother and community worker in a position to start searching for a way to ensure that the child receives both schooling and adequate nutrition.

Respect should be communicated through every aspect of the community worker's interaction with individuals in the community. At a structural and systemic level, respect is communicated by the amount of power that community representatives hold within the organisation, and in how the organisation responds to the varied concerns and suggestions arising from members of targeted communities. A member of the leadership forum commented: '*Survivors [KZN-PSV] are so good, because they help people to put their backs up straight again, and not feel ashamed because we are poor and black.*'

When members of targeted communities expect community workers to assist them with a daunting array of problems, but remain trapped within their own deep sense of helplessness, an attitude of respect becomes increasingly difficult to sustain. An informed understanding of why people become helpless and overwhelmingly needy helps the community worker to be more effective, while at the same time sustaining the attitude of deep respect. For this reason too, regular and intense supervision of staff is important.

Accurate empathy

It is often taken for granted that effective practitioners empathise accurately and fully with survivors of violence. This assumption must be questioned. In fact, most practitioners are unlikely to comprehend either accurately or fully the experience of living from day to day with politically inspired violence, especially when the stress is combined with having to cope with poverty and discrimination. Thus accurate empathy is impossible unless practitioners treat their engagement with the community as an on-going learning experience. The goal of establishing empathic relationships must be enhanced through the careful selection of insightful staff who understand the socio-political complexities of the situations in which they will be working. Where personnel come from communities similar to those targeted by the organisation, accurate empathy may be more easily achieved.

Opportunities for emotional expression

In the face of overwhelming needs, there is a temptation to seek or impose quick solutions to problems. When field personnel begin to 'manage' communities in this way, opportunities for emotional expression are lost. Most often, emotional expression occurs in small groups or in individual dialogue with field staff. Good listening skills and the ability to create a supportive and containing relationship are important in this regard. Emotions can also find powerful expression through creative writing and drama (especially with adolescents and young adults), singing and prayer (with older adults), and through play and art (with children and adolescents). A poem written by Philisiwe Gomba of Inanda when she was 19 years old, which was published by KZN-PSV in a book entitled *On Common Ground* (Malange *et al.*, 1996), deals with women's experience of the violence and the need for emotional expression.

Cry your anguish and sorrow out

You are the mothers of the nations,
You are the pillars of our communities and our beloved homes,

Your capabilities are still wonders for us, for every time we turn around,
you seem to amaze us.

How come then, that you allow your goodness to be
Hidden by that tiny dark cloud.

Before you could even say HAWU!
all of your hard work will have vanished
Your silence is making you your own victim.

Climb the ladder into the top of the tower and cry out
your anguish and sorrow as loud as you can,
for the universe needs to hear your cries.

Your cries will brighten the dark cloud,
and only then will you be proud of being mothers of the nations,
Being mothers, that you are most blessed,
and that responsibility can't be taken away from you.

Opportunities for people to tell their stories

Retelling the central stories of personal and community life allows people to make sense of and organise their experiences in a way which makes them more manageable and less distressing. At the same time, having other people serve as witnesses to these stories serves to give them legitimacy and acceptance. This process is understood by both African and Western healers to be vital to the process of individual and communal healing.

A youth-group member had this to say about the effect on his life of unresolved and distressing memories:

> ❛ Until the desire and inspiration to go forward becomes stronger than the memories of the past experiences, you will never hold the power to move forward with your life and keep focused to achieve your goals. ❜

Opportunities for people to change their beliefs about their world

It is crucial for community workers to understand that the violence inherent in civil conflict takes on particular meaning for survivors, and that it is largely this created meaning which determines the extent to which the community will disintegrate, survive, or thrive. Many individual victims of violence find that through surviving their victimisation they grow as people. Similarly, there are opportunities for communities to grow through surviving civil conflict.

The sense that members of the community make of the civil violence, and the way in which the community responds to that violence are both crucial. In order for constructive meaning to be created, it is important for members of the community to come together to express their views, and make their suggestions about how best to cope. Facilitating this sharing of views, ideas, and support, when the usual mechanisms of community functioning have been temporarily overwhelmed by the violence, is one of the most important roles that a service agency can play.

Collaborative relationships

Equal power sharing between the community agency and the target community is an ideal which is seldom achieved. However, it is important that everything is done to make the relationship as equitable as possible. Some suggestions based on the experience of the KZN-PSV are presented below.

- First, it is important that the service agency should respond only to explicit requests for assistance from community structures. In this way, the agency is invited into the community and does not enter without express permission.

- Second, community representatives must be included in the planning of any intervention strategies within the community. Apart from the obvious necessity of having people who are intimately aware of local dynamics involved in the planning process, this ensures that community structures take responsibility for projects from the beginning. Structurally, this can be achieved at two levels. At the local level, project committees, consisting of members of the community and field workers, are responsible for projects. At a regional level, community representatives are elected by their communities to sit on the Board of Directors of the KZN-PSV and participate in the management of all aspects of the work.

- Third, the community in general must be made aware of projects that are being started in the community. This involves public meetings, which are held regularly in many communities in KwaZulu-Natal, at which community representatives and field workers can introduce the proposed projects to the broader community.

Trust

Trust is usually considered critical to effective intervention. However, people in violence-torn areas have typically been betrayed and abandoned by more than one authority figure. On the road into one of the target communities in which the KZN-PSV works is a sign in Zulu which reads: *Trust Nobody*. Examples of betrayal by authority figures include parents who abandoned family members by leaving their homes to fight, or by being killed; teachers and principals who are too de-motivated to teach; local and regional political leaders who take children into paramilitary forces from which they sometimes do not return; priests, traditional leaders, and healers who are unable to provide protection and support in times of crisis; and members of the police and security forces, and justice personnel, who hold conventionally dependable and responsible positions, but who lost this status many years ago. As a result, it is necessary for field workers to demonstrate absolute trustworthiness.

Seemingly small things, such as attending every meeting and always being punctual, are very important. This sends a clear message that the framework for intervention is stable and the field workers are sincere. In evaluations of the KZN-PSV's interventions, community members have indicated that the constancy of the organisation's presence in an unstable community (particularly during upsurges of violence) is normalising and reassuring. Trustworthiness also requires strict adherence to the ethical codes of confidentiality, always working to assist the community, and never exploiting them.

Trust may be eroded if community members develop unrealistic expectations of what they can expect from the service agency. Helplessness is a characteristic of many communities that have been severely disrupted by civil violence. These communities may be resistant to service providers who do not offer them anything tangible. Community work must begin with the understanding that field workers are not responsible for the community's well-being, and that their role is to assist local people to resolve local concerns for themselves. Only by being very clear about what the agency can and cannot provide in the beginning will trust be sustained throughout the intervention.

Owing to the nature of community work in violence-torn areas, especially in the under-resourced non-government sector, the consistency and clarity required is sometimes very difficult to achieve. However, the repercussions of not continuously proving trustworthy can be very costly to the work. At a function to say goodbye to a long-standing staff member, an elder woman of Bhambayi made a speech to the community and the organisation's field workers in which she said that what for her was the most important thing about the KZN-PSV was that, even in the community's hardest times, they knew that their group meeting would run, and that our field workers would be there. Of all the work and projects in which we had been involved with this community, when it came to looking back, it was the fact that we had proved trustworthy that was most significant for her.

Working with small groups

Our experience with the KZN-PSV has taught us that small-group work is indispensable. When properly facilitated, small groups contain and express many of the diverse dynamics which exist between the participants. KZN-PSV works with groups of children, parents, community leaders, women, and young people, depending on the particular community. Membership of groups is open, with some people attending more regularly than others. Groups typically consist of between 15 and 25 individuals. It is essential for the group to be formed and developed in such a way that participants feel safe to discuss their feelings. In communities which have experienced a long history of violence, this is a slow process, which requires patience on the part of the facilitator. The usual group ethic of confidentiality is frequently challenged by family members, particularly by the men in the lives of the female group participants, who believe that they have a right to know what has been discussed, by virtue of both their status and their need to protect their womenfolk. The confidentiality code within a group therefore may create suspicious reactions from outsiders to the group process. Subjects under discussion can be extremely threatening, which carries the risk of rejection and further alienation for participants.

Facilitators must have the capacity to contain emotions generated in the group, in order for the members to feel safe in sharing their traumatic memories and the resultant experiences and emotions. Most people in communities which have experienced on-going violence have very little capacity to deal with either their own feelings or those of others, without feeling overwhelmed. Trust in the containing strength of the facilitator can be achieved only through a gradual process of testing. Thus it is likely that in earlier sessions relatively superficial issues will be raised, as these are 'safer' in emotional terms than the more traumatic incidents.

The content of group sessions is determined by the members themselves. Thus, for example, youth groups are likely to spend time working on issues of personal development (especially gaining employment and other skills), coping with unemployment, issues of sexuality (including HIV and AIDS), and so on. Community leaders spend more time discussing local problems, ways of obtaining resources for the community, and so forth. The women's groups focus on income-generating projects as well as relationships, parenting, substance abuse, and domestic violence. If specific expertise is required, beyond the competence of KZN-PSV personnel, other agencies are invited to run the groups; thus isolated communities can avail themselves of information and resources to which they would not normally have access.

Staff must be able to recognise the various patterns of relationships which can develop between members of groups, and between group members and facilitators. The facilitators run the risk of having group members become dependent upon them for emotional support. This in turn places facilitators in a powerful position and may make them feel needed and effective. This manner of relating does not, however, prepare the group members for emotional self-sufficiency when the facilitator is no longer present.

Similarly, group members may express anger, sadness, hopelessness, fear, frustration, and distrust in their relationship with the group facilitator, and it is important for the community worker to be able to make accurate judgements about the causes behind these feelings. The natural human response in the face of such emotions can take a number of forms. Emotions can be internalised and cause the staff member to become overwhelmed with a sense of extreme futility: it is now well known that one of the core predictors of secondary traumatic stress is the feeling of helplessness that accompanies much work in extremely impoverished communities. Or the staff member may be stirred into the non-productive responses of assuming power, installing facilities, running projects and events – in other words, working in a way which perpetuates the disempowerment and fragmentation of the community. The third possible human response is the dramatically increased likelihood of burn-out. Supervision, support, and enjoyable events for staff are essential elements of any programme in order to sustain their motivation, enthusiasm, and drive.

Honesty and transparency

In a community which is at war with itself, it is often very difficult to differentiate truth from lies. People living under these conditions learn to be extremely suspicious of what people tell them, and will try to authenticate the information in order to protect themselves. It is, therefore, essential that field workers and facilitators are entirely transparent about the smallest of details. This is often not as easy as it sounds, when working in a highly politicised community full of diverse and opposing concerns.

Ways of ensuring honesty and transparency include ensuring that detailed written notes are kept of all meetings and distributed to all stakeholders, in the interests of shared understanding. Structures which allow community members to observe and influence the decision making of the service provider should also be established. For example, representatives of target communities sit on the management committee of KZN-PSV, and everyone involved in the organisation's work is invited to attend an annual general meeting, at which the organisation's finances are publicly discussed.

In addition, facilitators must be clear about the constraints on their own resources (often imposed by their funders, parent organisations, and other structures) and about the limits of their skills and experience. Acknowledging that staff do not have the requisite skills to help with income-generating projects, or the resources to pay volunteers, prevents false expectations being raised.

Building on existing strengths and coping strategies

The community spirit of many of the people with whom we work needs to be supported, respected, and developed. Cultural traditions, in non-corrupted forms, should be explored as possible mechanisms for adaptive coping. African societies have survived many trials in the past and they have a variety of traditions and rituals which facilitate coping. Such traditions must form the foundation of intervention strategies, but they are seldom sufficient in themselves. This is because so many traditions have been corrupted through Westernisation and industrialisation and no longer effectively fulfil their original functions. For example, traditional leaders (including *amakhozi* and *indunas*) hold power and authority over many rural communities, and yet the people who depend on their goodwill enjoy no legal protection from any abuse of power that may occur. Many South Africans are ambivalent about the wisdom, impartiality, and authority of the traditional leadership of their community.

The transitional state of society is a further corrosive ingredient in traditional culture. The speed with which change is coming to urban and peri-urban communities in South Africa creates an enormous gulf between parents and children. Rebuilding relationships between people of different generations is a slow and painful process, but a very important one.

Christianity is another important factor which has affected traditional life. Although its proponents are largely responsible for some communities abandoning their traditional belief systems, Christianity also provides a strong spiritual anchor for many individuals. The human-rights work of some church organisations has increased their credibility as institutions which serve the people. Churches have offered refuge and conducted various healing services. However, some Christian teaching encourages a fatalistic approach to life, which requires believers to 'bear the cross' of suffering. An uncritical acceptance of either traditional or religious healing mechanisms does not take into account the complexities of the individual search for healing.

Practitioners need to help people to discriminate more effectively between what does and does not assist them as individuals and as communities.

Respect for local culture

Demonstrating respect for individuals and community structures entails respect for the cultural norms prevalent within that community. It is not true that communities are culturally homogeneous. In fact, a range of differing cultures exists within target communities, as in society at large. For example, the values, beliefs, and practices of young people who left school to participate in civil conflict are different from those of their parents and grandparents. Many of the communities in which the KZN-PSV works include people of more than one language group and ethnic background. Many Zulu people in KwaZulu-Natal are imbued with racial prejudices about Pondo people – prejudices which are reminiscent of those that some white South Africans entertain about black people. It is also important to observe that different political structures develop different cultures. In KwaZulu-Natal, the ANC structures are founded upon the ideal of democratic participation, and so young people in ANC-dominated communities find it easy to participate in workshops and tend to be relatively confident and skilled. The IFP structures, on the other hand, are founded on the ideals of traditional norms such as respect for elders, and so younger people in IFP-dominated communities often find it more difficult to participate fully in the workshops.

Also, very few individuals can be characterised as belonging to a single culture. Most people exist between cultures, drawing from each what seems appropriate for the reality of their lives. For example, although the majority of people in rural KwaZulu-Natal are Christians and attend church regularly, most still perform ceremonies honouring their ancestors, consult *sangomas*, and hold a range of beliefs about the cosmos that are in no way Christian in their origin.

Considering cultural differences in terms of the theory of post-traumatic stress, we find that although there are some differences in patterns of symptomatology, there are also many similarities. However, the *meaning* that is attributed to the traumatic experiences and the experience of the symptoms can be strikingly different. For example, at a settlement of displaced people in the South Coast region of KwaZulu-Natal, many people reported nightmares relating to attacks and the resultant massacres to which the community had been subjected. In terms of 'Western' traumatic-stress theory, this would be understood as an intrusive re-experiencing of the trauma. The shared understanding of people in the community, however, was that these dreams were warnings of future attacks. If as a practitioner one is able to identify one's own assumptions and beliefs about people, the world, society, distress, health, and healing, one can begin to work in a way which demonstrates respect for culture.

Safety

The final guiding principle of community work in contexts prone to civil violence is the all-important question of safety. Developmental work cannot begin until relative peace has returned to a community, but it is often the case that a resurgence in violence occurs. At this time the community workers and their supervisors are faced with a difficult dilemma: is it better to discontinue support at a time when communities need it most, or to risk the safety of staff working in a potentially dangerous situation? This dilemma is often compounded if staff have a great emotional investment in their work within communities and become angry when told that they cannot continue for an indefinite period. But the safety of staff must always come first.

Where people are working under dangerous conditions, the stress is multiplied, and the chances of secondary traumatic stress and burn-out rise exponentially. However, this does not mean that target communities must be abandoned. The KZN-PSV has developed appropriate strategies for supporting communities that are suffering from continuing violence. The organisation has often resorted to transporting large groups of people from their communities to the safety of its offices in the cities of Durban and Pietermaritzburg, in order that regular meetings and projects can continue, despite the prevailing violence. This has enormous financial implications, but it is one important way of sustaining contact with a community. In addition, it is almost always possible to get messages into and out of communities. The knowledge that people in the outside world are aware of the situation and will be there in support when the possibility arises is enough to give people hope.

A final word of caution regarding violence and safety. It is often the case that violent incidents within a particular community increase gradually. Without any clear 'declaration of war', it may be difficult for supervisors to judge when the threat is so great as to warrant withdrawing the community workers. Accurate and sensitive information is necessary to this decision-making process, and thus this work requires community workers and their supervisors to operate with their eyes and ears wide open. It is easy to become desensitised to violence, and so the threat seems less than it actually is. The best way of dealing with this problem is to use people whose judgement has not been prejudiced by over-exposure to violence to support and assess the difficult choices that must be made.

Long-term care of the organisation and its personnel

Long-term work in communities that have been severely damaged by civil violence is often extremely disheartening. Change comes slowly, and sudden upsurges of violence may in one night destroy the progress made over several months. Unless actively managed, the stress of the work can easily destroy the organisation, or the individuals who comprise it.

In the mid-1990s a number of books were written about secondary traumatic stress (alternatively named 'vicarious traumatisation' and 'compassion fatigue'). These books recognised the enormous price that community workers may pay for the work that they do, unless adequately cared for by the structure in which they function. In the words of a member of the KZN-PSV staff: '*It has not been easy to listen to all these painful stories. When people talk, I see in my mind what they see, and it stays with me afterwards.*' The KZN-PSV, like many other organisations that work in situations of violence and trauma, has struggled with problems of secondary traumatic stress since its inception. That these problems are properly addressed is crucial to the long-term sustainability of the work.

Like the work in communities, effective management of secondary traumatic stress within the organisation requires intervention at multiple levels. These levels include those of the organisation, the team, and the individual.

Organisational intervention

When mental-health workers find themselves working under conditions of continuous threat, it is very easy for them to start seeing themselves as a kind of fearless paramilitary force, fighting for the cause of mental health. A certain level of denial becomes inevitable; but this can be extremely dangerous if it results in irresponsible decisions which put personnel at unacceptable risk. Further, when a climate of denial develops within an organisation, staff are discouraged from experiencing and expressing their own distress in the face of the threat and suffering to which their work exposes them. An organisational climate which encourages honest self-monitoring and the expression of distress is important, and can be achieved through the following measures.

- Staff should be educated about the risks to their own mental health. They should understand that, unless adequately managed, the high level of traumatic exposure that they experience will inevitably result in secondary traumatic stress, a condition which is extremely distressing and debilitating, and more difficult to treat than other forms of traumatic stress.

- People should never be discouraged from expressing their distress. It is important to develop a climate where staff can talk about their experiences and emotions without feeling that it will in any way damage their standing in the eyes of their colleagues and supervisor.

- When staff do not manage their emotions appropriately, it is important that this behaviour be corrected in a supportive manner, sensitive to the difficulty of managing feelings in this type of context. In one situation in the organisation's history, the facilitator of a youth group became exceptionally frustrated and lost her temper with a group of young people, who despite her work had allowed themselves to be drawn into another bout of fighting in their community. Helping this community worker to understand her anger, in particular its basis in the very realistic fear that members of her youth group would die violently, was successful in changing her emotional and behavioural response to a very difficult situation.

- By putting the issue of staff health on the agenda of every meeting, an awareness of secondary traumatic stress grows within the agency. In most cases it was an item that was passed over with comments like 'Yes, we're all doing fine this week', but at other times it saved us from sending vulnerable people into stressful situations.

- It is important to have clear regulations to govern the work of staff members. The staff of the KZN-PSV are deeply emotionally involved with members of the communities where they are working, and in many cases community workers are resistant to the instruction to take time off for recreation. This is particularly true when the immediate situation in their target communities is unstable; but staff must take their allocated leave.

- Many staff feel that they should be allowed to make personal decisions about their own safety at work. This is not sensible. Personnel struggling with secondary traumatic stress are likely to make poor judgements about whether to enter a community where civil violence currently prevails, and they make take unacceptable risks. In KZN-PSV, the decision is made by the director of the organisation (who is not working as regularly within particular target communities), in discussion with community workers.

- Organisational structure is also important. Within KZN-PSV, every staff member is part of a team, and team dynamics are constantly monitored to produce a supportive work environment. Also job descriptions must be suitably varied to create space away from the field for staff to deal with traumatic experiences, both individually and in groups.

Intervention at the team level
The structure of KZN-PSV depends on teams working in various communities. They typically consist of between two and five members, and a senior, highly

skilled, and experienced person serves as team leader and supervisor. The team leader is expected to manage his or her team in a way that maintains a high level of morale and support. This is best achieved through celebrating team successes in a very public way, employing strongly participative management methods, and fostering a high level of personal sharing and trust within teams. But team members are also responsible for monitoring each other's welfare and looking out for signs of traumatic stress. In most cases, team members approach colleagues who seem to be in need of support, and persuade them to seek help. Cases in which members of staff do not wish to acknowledge their own levels of secondary traumatic stress are handled through the team leader.

Individual interventions

Finally, and most importantly, all staff are responsible for monitoring their own social and psychological health, and for seeking support when they need it. It has happened that staff ignore or actively hide the effects that their work is having on them, in order not to have to confront the pain of the experience. In precisely the same way that community members avoid confronting the pain of traumatic experiences, so community workers often resist confronting the pain and distress that they experience as a result of their work.

Secondary traumatic stress tends to be explained away as 'working too hard', 'being tired', or 'suffering from burn-out'. However, the differences between secondary traumatic stress and burn-out are very clear: while the latter may be effectively dealt with by taking a holiday or reducing work loads, secondary traumatic stress may lead to lasting clinical depression and other very serious long-term consequences.

Although secondary traumatic stress is a virtually inevitable consequence of working for extended periods of time in communities experiencing high levels of violence, this problem is easily managed, provided that staff remain aware of the dangers and act continually to protect and strengthen themselves.

Final thoughts

The most important question in the end is whether or not, through all the efforts of the people involved with the KZN-PSV, there has been some positive change in the communities with which we have worked. Levels of conflict are lower than they have been in two decades; new community structures exist and are making observable progress in developing their areas; new economic opportunities have opened up within many communities; and the current

generation of young people is largely in school. These positive changes are
due to multiple factors, not least of which are the elections of 1994 and the
agreements reached between the ANC and IFP since that date. But if you ask
the community representatives who work with KZN-PSV on a daily basis, the
members of the projects being run by the organisation, or the organisation's
community workers, the response is unanimous: the work of the KZN-PSV
has contributed significantly to the current stability and relative health of
communities who bore the brunt of civil violence in KwaZulu-Natal.
The following words of thanks were written by Jabu Zikhali, a member of one
of the organisation's youth groups.

> I feel like singing a song!
> I feel like dancing!
> Because of you KwaZulu-Natal Programme for Survivors of Violence!
> ...
> Again I say thank you!
> I wish you all the best!
> Long Live KwaZulu-Natal Programme for Survivors of Violence.

In the end, the successes of the KZN-PSV are not due to our reproducing what
other agencies working in similar situations have done. They have been due
to our efforts to develop deep relationships with individuals and structures
within the local communities. Through these relationships, we as helpers are
able to understand the immediate and more distant concerns of our intended
beneficiaries, and as a result we can respond more meaningfully. In short, the
work of the KZN-PSV is successful for the following reasons:

- the organisation commits itself to working hard, and over a long period of
  time, with particular communities;
- the work is thoughtful and strategic at all times;
- our community workers adhere strictly to fundamental principles of
  community work;
- and because as an organisation we take good care of our own.

This book was written not in the hope that other agencies working in situations
of civil conflict will try to replicate what we have done, but that they will
consider adopting KZN-PSV's approach to the communities that it continues
to assist.

Thanks to you
I was floating in sorrow,
I couldn't think about tomorrow
I was scared to face the future,
'cause my past was too full of sorrow.

You came along as true friends
You wiped away my tears
You chased away my fears
You washed away my pain
You swallowed my sorrow and
You brought back my hope

You named me 'survivor of violence'
Something about that name
It puts me on the right path
Knowing I follow your footsteps
It ensures me a better future
Knowing I have you by my side
It makes me strong
Knowing you among me it won't be wrong.

You're so special to me
You're so sympathetic to my problems
You're so comforting to my pain
You're so healing to my heartache
You're a companion to my loneliness
You wear my shoes and
You never complain about pain.

I roll a red carpet for you all
May God bless you all
Be proud and walk tall
Thanks to you all.

(Ntokozo Ndlovu, November 1999)

Bibliography

Arden, N. (1996) *The Spirits Speak: One Woman's Mystical Journey into the African Spirit World,* New York: Henry Holt and Company

Bless, C. and R. C. Higson-Smith (2000) *Fundamentals of Social Research Merthods: An African Perspective* (Third Edition), Cape Town: Juta

Bronfenbrenner, U. (1979) *The Ecology of Human Development: Experiments by Nature and Design,* Cambridge, MA: Harvard University Press

Campbell, S. S. (1998) *Called to Heal: Traditional Healing Meets Modern Medicine in Southern Africa Today,* Johannesburg: Zebra

Chikane, F. (1986) 'The effects of the unrest on township children', in S. Burman and P. Reynolds (eds.) *Growing Up in a Divided Society,* Illinois: Northwestern Press.

Cock, J. and L. Nathan (1989) *War and Society: The Militarisation of South Africa,* Cape Town: David Philip

Coleman, M. (ed.) (1998) *A Crime Against Humanity: Analysing the Repression of the Apartheid State,* Cape Town: David Philip

Dawes, A. and D. Donald (eds.) (1994) *Childhood and Adversity: Psychological Perspectives from South African Research,* Cape Town: David Philip

Herman, J. (1992) 'Complex PTSD: a syndrome in survivors of prolonged and repeated trauma', *Journal of Traumatic Stress* 5: 377-420

Henderson, P. (1998) 'Tracing fragility in families: children's reflections on mobility in new Crossroads, Cape Town', *In View of School – Preparation for and Adjustment to School under Rapidly Changing Social Conditions,* Johannesburg: Goethe Institute

Higson-Smith, C. (1995) 'Dealing with Social Violence at Community Level: Experiences of the KwaZulu-Natal Programme for Survivors of Violence', paper presented at the Annual Congress of the Association of Children and Adolescent Psychiatry and Allied Professions

Higson-Smith, C. (1998) 'The Cost of Violence to Development', paper presented at the Conference on Political Violence in the KwaZulu-Natal Midlands, 1984–1994, University of Natal, Pietermaritzburg

Jeffery, A. (1997) *The Natal Story: Sixteen Years of Conflict,* Johannesburg: South African Institute of Race Relations

Kentridge, M. (1990) *An Unofficial War: Inside the Conflict in Pietermaritzburg*, Cape Town: David Philip

Malange, N., A. McKay, and Z. Nhlengetwa (1996) *On Common Ground*, Durban: KwaZulu-Natal Programme for Survivors of Violence

Mandela, N. (1994) *Long Walk to Freedom: The Autobiography of Nelson Mandela*, London: Abacus

Morgan, R. (1995) 'Children as a Development Issue: Implications for the Reconstruction and Development Programme', mimeo

Motala, S. (1997) 'Education', in. S. Robinson and L. Biersteker (eds.) *First Call: The South African Children's Budget*, Cape Town: IDASA

Mutwa, C. (1986) *Let Not My Country Die*, Pretoria: United Publishers International

Mutwa, V. C. (1996) *Song of the Stars: The Lore of a Zulu Shaman*, New York: Barrytown

Nicol, M. (1995) *The Waiting Country: A South African Witness*, London: Victor Gollancz

Reed, D. (1994) *Beloved Country: South Africa's Silent Wars*, Johannesburg, Jonathan Ball

Reynolds, P. (1995) 'Not known because not looked for: ethnographers listening to the young in Southern Africa', *Ethnos*, 60, 193-221

Reynolds, P. (1996) *Traditional Healers and Childhood in Zimbabwe*, Athens, Ohio: Ohio University Press

Roche, C. (1996) 'Operationality in turbulence: the need for change', in D. Eade (ed.) *Development in States of War*, Oxford: Oxfam GB

Rock, B. (ed.) (1997) *Spirals of Suffering: Public Violence and Children*, Pretoria: HSRC

Seidman, A. (1985) *The Roots of Crisis in Southern Africa*, New Jersey: Africa World Press

Sparks, A. (1990) *The Mind of South Africa: The Story of the Rise and Fall of Apartheid*, London: Heinemann

Straker, J. and F. Moosa (1994) 'Interacting with trauma survivors in contexts of continuing trauma', *Journal of Traumatic Stress*, 7:1-9

Summerfield, D. (1996) 'Assisting survivors of war and atrocity: notes on "psycho-social" issues for NGO workers', in D. Eade (ed.) *Development in States of War*, Oxford: Oxfam GB

Summerfield, D. (1999) 'A critique of seven assumptions behind psychological trauma programmes in war-affected areas', *Social Science and Medicine*, 48: 1449-62

Winter, R. (1987) *Action-Research and the Nature of Social Enquiry: Professional Innovation and Educational Work*, Aldershot: Avebury

Index